Make Bosses Pay

'An eloquent and accessible blend of history, theory, and practical advice, *Make Bosses Pay* is essential reading for the new working class. I want to hand this book to every young person starting out in work, and to a surprisingly large number of union leaders as well.'

—Sarah Jaffe, author of *Work Won't Love You Back*

'The pandemic has proved once again that unions are indispensable. Eve's book is a brilliant primer for people wanting to find out more about the movement and why they should join. But she is also clear throughout that unions could be doing more and better, particularly for the young workers who need them so badly in today's unfair economy.'

—Frances O'Grady, General Secretary of the Trades Union Congress (TUC)

'A brave manifesto for trade unions at a pivotal moment in our history, expressed through voices from the frontlines of that fight. Eve's bold vision sends a powerful message to any worker who feels disempowered and alone: that you are not alone, that you are a leader and that your time to lead is now.'

—Henry Chango Lopez, General Secretary, Independent Workers Union of Great Britain (IWGB)

Outspoken by Pluto
Series Editor: Neda Tehrani

Platforming underrepresented voices; intervening in important political issues; revealing powerful histories and giving voice to our experiences; Outspoken by Pluto is a book series unlike any other. Unravelling debates on feminism and class, work and borders, unions and climate justice, this series has the answers to the questions you're asking. These are books that dissent.

Also available:

Make Bosses Pay

Why We Need Unions

Eve Livingston

First published 2021 by Pluto Press
345 Archway Road, London N6 5AA

www.plutobooks.com

British Library Cataloguing in Publication Data
A catalogue record for this book is available from the British Library

ISBN   978 0 7453 4162 0   Paperback
ISBN   978 1 78680 840 0   PDF
ISBN   978 1 78680 841 7   EPUB

This book is printed on paper suitable for recycling and made from fully
managed and sustained forest sources. Logging, pulping and manufacturing processes are expected to conform to the environmental standards of
the country of origin.

Typeset by Stanford DTP Services, Northampton, England

Simultaneously printed in the United Kingdom and United States of
America

Contents

Acknowledgements

Firstly, thank you to my editor Neda Tehrani for all her wisdom, encouragement and patience, and for making this book into something much better than I ever could have managed on my own. And thanks to everyone at Pluto for their support in bringing this book to life.

Thank you to all who shared their experiences, expertise and analysis with me. Your insights helped me immeasurably in shaping this book and articulating its vision. Thank you to Dawn Butler, Clare Coatman, Jaime Cross, Anny Cullum, Jo Grady, Josephine Grahl, Simon Hannah, Nicole Moore, Emma Saunders, Melanie Simms, Bryan Simpson, Fran Scaife, Tam Wilson, John Wood, Jamie Woodcock, Becky Wright, Amy and Esme, and to everyone else I spoke to whose words aren't directly quoted but whose contributions are still evident throughout.

There were so many people who helped me whether they knew it or not, by reading through proposals, sections and chapters, answering my questions, introducing me to others, or simply being brilliantly supportive and patient friends, colleagues and family. Thank you to Alex Collinson, Lucy Douglas, Gillian Furmage, E Jamieson, Eleanor Livingston, James Mackenzie, Calum Macleod, Màiri Macleod, Carla McCormack, Emiliano Mellino, Zeyn Mohammed, Elliot Ross, Kane Shaw, Laura Waddell, Hannah Walters and Hannah Westwater – and to any others I have undoubtedly missed out but who I promise I'm just as grateful to.

ACKNOWLEDGEMENTS

There are three people who deserve more thanks than I can give them on this page. Thank you to Nicole Busby, who instilled in me all the values I've poured onto these pages, and who shaped this book immensely with both her insights and her support. To Dash Peruvamba, who has always been my number one champion and the best friend I could ask for, and who read every chapter with unerring patience and enthusiasm. And to Sean Kippin, for everything.

Introduction

I first joined a trade union when I was 22 years old. I'd graduated a year previously, spent the interim period cutting my teeth in the union movement as vice-president of my students' union, and was ready to enter the world of work. Lifelong union membership was part and parcel of the deal for me, as obvious and unremarkable a feature of working life as rush hour commutes, tepid canteen coffee and hours-long meetings that could definitely just be emails. The union representatives at my workplace, a large public sector organisation with a relatively strong and active union, took a different view. At an induction session on my first day, after a five-minute presentation about the union, one rep spent double that time wooing my fellow inductees – both largely disinterested white men older than me – before remarking that I probably wouldn't be interested in union membership. Of the three, I was the one with union experience, shared principles and an eagerness to join. But apparently, I didn't look the type.

I signed up regardless, and ultimately got along with my fellow members and reps – even after one tried to make it up to me by delivering to my office an unmarked brown envelope containing a pot of shoe polish branded with a union logo five years out of date and apparently left over from a recruitment drive in the 1980s. But my baptism into the trade union movement is still illustrative of many of its enduring problems and the stereotypes that continue to deter young workers from joining today: unions are for shouty old white men. They're stuck in the past and don't have any power left. It's an old-fashioned model that doesn't fit the way we work now. And to some extent, there is truth in all of the above. Workers from marginalised groups have fought hard for their place at the table and can still be found having to fight throughout the movement. Decades of Conservative legislation have weakened unions and removed much of their power. The world of work has changed beyond all recognition since the heyday of the movement in post-war Britain. And yet, trade unionism remains one of the strongest weapons we have in a country where inequality is accelerating, and work isn't working. Young people in today's United Kingdom are the first generation to be poorer than the one before,[1] and a pension, let alone a home of our own, seems like a pipedream. We're at the sharp end of changes to the workplace, more likely than any other demographic to be stuck on zero-hour contracts or inside the precarious gig economy,[2] and some of the most vulnerable to discrimination and bullying at work.[3] As I write this introduction, the country is still grappling with the consequences of the Coronavirus pandemic, but the disproportionate impact on young people's jobs and income is already clear, with more than one in three 18- to 24-year-olds earning less than before the outbreak, and a higher percentage of job losses than any other age group.[4] If today's cruel, unequal country and its ruthless workplaces have taught us anything, it's that the powerful won't save us. But collectivism still might.

---

1 https://ft.com/content/81343d9e-187b-11e8-9e9c-25c814761640 (last accessed April 2021).

2 https://ons.gov.uk/employmentandlabourmarket/peopleinwork/earningsand workinghours/articles/contractsthatdonotguaranteeaminimumnumberofhours/ april2018#future-of-the-experimental-business-survey (last accessed April 2021).

3 https://unison.org.uk/get-help/knowledge/vulnerable-workers/young-workers/ (last accessed April 2021).

4 https://bbc.co.uk/news/business-52717942 (last accessed April 2021).

Who are young workers?

Young workers are not a homogenous group and attempts to strictly define them as such can be largely arbitrary. In the course of writing this book, for example, I turned 28 and instantly aged out of eligibility for the young workers' structures of many unions. Others draw their lines differently or are in the process of doing so, mindful that austerity and accelerating inequality have seen us become independent later than in previous generations, and that the problems facing young people at work are often the same as those plaguing their older counterparts. When I talk about young workers in this book, then, I define them loosely as anyone with a job under the age of around 30 – encompassing both the younger end of 'millennial', and what has come to be known as 'Gen Z'.[5] But in doing so I acknowledge two things: first, that those who fit that definition exist across all sectors, pay grades, workplaces, geographical locations, social identities and life circumstances. Some young workers live with their parents; some *are* parents; some are students; some have been working for decades; some benefit from and inherit generational wealth; some are well-paid and secure; some earn less than minimum wage and their jobs are precarious. And secondly, that those who don't fit that definition might still identify as young workers and will almost certainly find many of the insights, testimonies and lessons in this book applicable to their own circumstances and work lives. I focus on young workers not as an intellectual exercise in defining and siphoning off one section of the movement, but as one lens through which to view that movement – and because these

5   https://pewresearch.org/fact-tank/2019/01/17/where-millennials-end-and-generation-z-begins/ (last accessed April 2021).

workers will ultimately come to inherit and transform it in the future.

The changing world of work and political tumult of recent years has left young workers especially exposed and vulnerable. We're working longer, for less, in jobs more insecure than any generation before us and with a future much less certain than theirs, too. We're at the whim of bad bosses, threats from technological advances, ruthless government policy – and we're also the least likely of any demographic to be part of a union. In fact, membership has fallen by almost 50 per cent among 16- to 24-year-olds and 35 per cent for 25- to 30-year-olds in the past 25 years.[6] In 2017, only 2 per cent of 16- to 19-year-old were members of a trade union.[7] This reflects a general trend in union membership: in 2017, the movement experienced its biggest ever drop in numbers, losing 275,000 members and seeing membership decrease to 6.2 million.[8] While numbers have subsequently risen – including throughout the Coronavirus pandemic – they have not, at the time of writing, yet made up for that loss.

This combination of high vulnerability and low union density (that is, trade union members as a percentage of employees) leaves young workers more isolated than ever within the quickly changing and complex web of work, just how capitalism wants us. Navigating workplace culture as individuals rather than in the collective means that we face challenges alone, forced to perceive our peers as competitors rather than allies, and building our own personal management strategies instead of looking to a

6   Figures courtesy of the TUC.

7   http://classonline.org.uk/docs/TU_and_Inequality_for_print_18th_September.pdf (last accessed April 2021).

8   https://theguardian.com/politics/2017/jun/01/union-membership-has-plunged-to-an-all-time-low-says-ons (last accessed April 2021).

union to collectivise our experience. The scale of the threats we face is increasingly too big to be met on an individual level, and yet increasingly that's where we're told to look.

Young people aren't taking their lot lying down. The last few years have seen an eruption in discussions about 'side hustles' and workplace culture which follow both the changes outlined above as well as high profile scandals such as the #MeToo movement and enduring pay gaps at institutions like the BBC. The result has been a proliferation of podcasts, panel events and soul-searching magazine columns (Why are more young people freelancing? What can we do if we're sexually harassed in the workplace? How can we ask for fairer pay?), in which unions are almost never mentioned. Instead, we're told, we should ask bosses nicely, do some deep breaths before a salary negotiation and consider escalating any grievances to HR. For reasons which we'll explore throughout this book, these are solutions which put the onus for change onto us as individuals without any collective power behind us, and to do nothing to challenge the inherent imbalance between workers and their employers.

Still fighting

It's a good job, then, that unions continue to weather the storm. In 2011, tens of thousands of public sector workers took part in what the TUC described as 'the biggest strike in a generation'[9] against pension changes. In 2016, junior doctors in England smashed the draconian restrictions of the Trade Union Act when 76 per cent of members turned out to vote 98 per cent in favour of the first general strike across the NHS in 40 years.[10] And in Glasgow in 2018, as we will discuss in Chapter 4, 8,000 low-paid

9   https://bbc.co.uk/news/uk-15953806
10   https://fullfact.org/health/did-98-junior-doctors-vote-strike/

women – cooks, cleaners and care workers – secured payouts worth hundreds of millions of pounds in the country's biggest equal pay strike action since the introduction of the Equal Pay Act in 1970.[11]

Across the country, and against a backdrop of attacks by governments and CEOs alike, dedicated activists and organisers continue to fight tirelessly for fair pay, conditions and dignity for the UK's 32 million workers. And key among them are young people, making their voices heard on the issues that affect them and their peers while bringing creative new ideas and energy to a movement that so badly needs it. From groundbreaking campaigns against zero-hour contracts to the establishment of new unions fighting for those in the gig economy, trade unionists are responding to the changes affecting young workers. From joining climate strikes to inspiring tenant organising across the UK, unions are battling not just for fair work in the present but for a future that young people – and all people – can feel secure about. Whether through diverse members unapologetically taking up space or organisers working tirelessly to bring trade unionism into the digital age, the movement can evolve into something that represents the reality of young workers' lives today.

And also underpinning all the arguments, testimonies and case studies throughout this book is an acknowledgement of something more personal and more boundless: the notion that involvement in a union – the skills gained, the bonds formed, the power built – can be just as important as the winning of campaigns and demands. Persistent on the left is a natural and justified suspicion of 'careerism', hierarchy and individualism, which are, after all, the antitheses to collective power and shared

11 https://theguardian.com/society/2019/jan/17/glasgow-council-women-workers-win-12-year-equal-pay-battle (last accessed April 2021).

interests. There are undoubtedly those who have sought to use the union movement as a springboard for their own profiles or to concentrate their own power in exactly the ways unions exist to fight. But we can make a distinction between building power for power's sake and building it as a means to further reproduce it. The former is a waste of time, resources and energy and an affront to union values; the latter is an imperative.

Trade unionists rightfully talk constantly about the role that unions can play in the workplace, and often about the one they have in a wider struggle for social justice. But less discussed are the lifelong impacts they can have on their members at the most personal level. As training grounds for political education and organising, unions are invaluable in creating the activists and leaders of the future. As brokers of lifelong learning, they can transform fortunes and present opportunities to those who may never have otherwise had them. As sites of socialising and support, they can cultivate friendships for life and engender the confidence and belief that capitalism would rather beat out of us. And as a force for working-class interests, they can shape a society that lets working-class people thrive in all arenas.

As this book will show, the situation for young workers in the UK is dire and worsening, and only unions hold the key to transforming it. By building solidarity between workers of all generations, they can create the strong base needed to take on capital. As part of an international workers' rights movement, they even have the potential to transform class relations and systems of exploitation globally. But they can't do it without the energy and input of young people themselves, speaking truth to power, bringing union organising into the present day, and transforming the movement from the inside. As we'll explore, young workers urgently need unions – and unions urgently need us.

Chapter 1

Why unions?

Have you ever had a boss who bullied or sexually harassed you, or who ignored your complaint when another member of staff did? How about one who faked your payslips and kept your tax contributions for themselves? Or who rejected your request for leave while your mother was dying, or while you were having a mental health crisis? Who wouldn't turn up the heating when the office was freezing? A boss who paid you less than your colleagues and then said you weren't a team player when you complained? One who refused you shifts and then fired you for not working enough hours? Who demanded you arrive ten minutes early and penalised you for leaving on time, despite paying you below minimum wage and by the hour? Who sacked you after seven years of service in the midst of a global pandemic? Who paid you so little you had to claim benefits and use food banks? Who put you under so much pressure you drove your car into a tree in an attempt to take your own life?

These are not extreme examples cooked up to misrepresent the boss class by focussing on a few 'bad apples': they are real-life experiences recounted to me by a range of workers of different backgrounds and in different sectors throughout the course of researching and writing this book – and they only scratch the surface of the egregious power abuses that unions and their members confront on a daily basis. If you haven't personally been mistreated at work, your friend, sibling, parent, partner or colleague has. This kind of conflict is a feature of work. The interests of bosses and workers are not just different but opposed, and in a constant tug of war: we need to sell our labour at a rate that allows us to live a decent life, while they want to extract it at as low a price as possible, for as big a gain as possible. We rely on them for survival but we're just one of many interchangeable and disposable workers they can pick up and drop as it suits them. Workers are the largest group in society, but power is concentrated with bosses; they choose how much to cede to you. The cards are always stacked in their favour. Marx wrote of this dynamic when he defined 'labour-power' as a worker's capacity to produce goods and services. It is this which a worker sells to the capitalist class, the owners of the means of production, who gain from their purchase not just the labour but the products of it too. This is capital: the accumulation of profit at the expense of the working class who produce it.[1]

Because we're indoctrinated into the world of waged labour from childhood – watching parents go to work each day; taking on Saturday and after-school jobs for pocket money; constantly being asked what we want to 'be' when we grow up and knowing instinctively it's a question about paid work – it can seem like an inevitable and obvious feature of society. But take a step back for a moment and consider that our workplaces, where we spend one third of our lives[2] toiling to prop up the other third not spent sleeping,[3] can also be the places where we're most in danger,

---

1 Karl Marx and James Leigh Joynes, *Wage-labour and capital* (Twentieth Century Press, 1893).

2 https://who.int/occupational_health/publications/globstrategy/en/index2. html#:~:text=Introduction%3A%20The%20right%20to%20health,their%20 families%20and%20of%20society (last accessed November 2020).

3 https://researchgate.net/publication/262060840_We_spend_about_one-third_ of_our_life_either_sleeping_or_attempting_to_do_so (last accessed November 2020).

where we're most exploited, where we're least in control. One of the relationships which has the most control over our lives is also one of the most fundamentally imbalanced.

Put simply, this is why we unionise. As individuals against capital, we're largely disposable, replaceable and, ultimately, powerless. But the reverse is true of a collective working class; the bosses rely on us to make their profits. Collectivism shifts this power dynamic, clawing back some control from capitalism's gatekeepers to those of us at its mercy.

The British labour movement: A potted history

Precisely because of their radicalism and potential for transformation, the history of trade unions has been long, messy and filled with challenges. Trade unions in the UK largely have their roots in the Industrial Revolution of the late eighteenth and early nineteenth centuries. Prior to this period, Britain's economy was an agricultural and handicraft one, with waged labour mainly consisting of manual work on farms and manufacturing by hand. But the advent of new technologies – not least steam power and the increasing use of mechanised tools and factory systems – saw a shift towards industrial work and the growth of new industries such as textiles and factory manufacturing. With this change came disputes about pay and conditions; while work itself became more regimented and defined, regulation was slower to follow and workers increasingly began to join forces to agitate for shorter hours and higher wages.[4] The Conservative government were quick to crack down on any sign of dissent, introducing the Combination Acts of 1799

4 http://homepages.gac.edu/~kranking/DigitalHistory/HIS321/HIS_321/W1.html (last accessed April 2021).

and 1800[5] to outlaw all forms of strike action. And it was easy for them to do so, given that the government at the time was elected only by landowning men, who amounted to around 3 per cent of the entire population.[6]

Despite the draconian response of the powerful, organising and activism were widespread during this time. The Combinations Acts were repealed in 1824 after campaigning by tailor and working-class activist Francis Place with support from the radical MP Joseph Hume. Following their abolishment, workers tried to form legal unions with mandated powers. Trade unionists of the time aimed to transcend industry divisions, opting instead to unite workers of all stripes under one broad banner. Their most famous attempt came in the form of the Grand National Consolidated Trades Union of 1833, a union which was short-lived, but which is still memorialised today – most notably because it was home to the Tolpuddle Martyrs, a group of six male labourers targeted for their union links and found guilty of 'administering illegal oaths' in a sham trial. Despite being convicted and deported to Australia, a widespread working-class backlash eventually saw the charges dropped and the sentences commuted, three years after the initial sentencing.[7]

In the latter part of the nineteenth century, many trade union leaders become politicised through the Chartism movement, a working-class campaign for political reform, but one which, unlike unions, pursued change via constitutional methods. Although their list of demands,[8] which pertained to working

---

5   https://britannica.com/event/Combination-Acts (last accessed November 2020).

6   http://nationalarchives.gov.uk/pathways/citizenship/struggle_democracy/getting_vote.htm (last accessed November 2020).

7   https://tolpuddlemartyrs.org.uk/story (last accessed November 2020).

8   https://parliament.uk/about/living-heritage/transformingsociety/elections voting/chartists/overview/chartistmovement/ (last accessed November 2020).

conditions, pay and other work-related issues, was never met, it ignited something in many activists who went on to grow and strengthen the trade union movement. By the 1860s, more permanent union bodies were becoming established, most notably the London Trades Union Council in 1860 and the Trades Union Congress in 1868.

Following the legalisation of trade unions and strike action in the Trade Union Act 1871, it was in the run up to the First World War that the movement really hit its stride, with unprecedented growth and strike action in the period 1888–1914, as well as major shifts in the internal make-up of unions. While previous iterations of trade unionism had seen schisms develop between so-called 'skilled' and 'unskilled' workers, the former of whom had often argued that they deserved better terms and conditions than the latter, the movement now largely focussed on uniting all workers within their industries. And though it would be a long time before women and other minoritised groups were given equal status within the movement (something many are still fighting for today), this period saw important victories such as the 1888 'match girl strike' at London's Bryant & May Factory, which saw women and teenage girls defeat their bosses over managerial and safety concerns, and the 1889 London Dock Strike in which 30,000 striking members won concessions from their employers on pay and conditions.[9] In 1900, trade unions teamed up with socialist campaign groups and political think tank the Fabian Society to found what we now know as the Labour Party. Its mission was clear: to advance the interests of labour within the structures of parliament. It would go on to do this in profound ways, not least through the establishment of the welfare state and National Health Service.

---

9 https://britannica.com/event/London-Dock-Strike (last accessed November 2020).

The outbreak of World War I in 1914 saw unions across the country leveraging their strength behind the war effort, but notable divisions in the labour movement also emerged in opposition to the bloody conflict: in Glasgow, Scotland, for example, the radical Red Clydeside coalition presented a strong working-class resistance to participation in the war. The years preceding the conflict had seen widespread unrest and strike action in the area, reflected in increasing trade union membership, and key Red Clydeside figures went on to lead historic rent strikes and the campaign for a 40-hour week.

While grassroots working-class activists continued to push this kind of militant action in the war's aftermath, the Great Depression it left behind also meant high unemployment and, consequently, decreased union membership. Attempts for radical action between the first and second world wars were often quashed. The TUC called for a General Strike in 1926 in support of disgruntled coalminers, but failed. In 1927, the later-repealed Trades Dispute and Trade Union Act outlawed sympathetic strikes and mass picketing. It was in the aftermath of World War II that unions peaked in membership and power. The nationalisation policies of the Labour government made the state a huge employer, and with it more women and migrants entered the workforce than ever before. Unions grew steadily, reaching their zenith in the 1970s and securing important wins such as equal pay for women.[10] And then came the Winter of Discontent. Widespread public sector strikes were called in 1978 and 1979, in response to pay caps introduced by James Callaghan's Labour government in an attempt to control inflation.

---

10   https://striking-women.org/module/workplace-issues-past-and-present/ gender-pay-gap-and-struggle-equal-pay (last accessed November 2020).

More than 29 million working days were lost to strike action,[11] and the inability of Callaghan's government to put an end to the strikes swept Margaret Thatcher's Conservatives to victory in 1979, paving the way for the most devastating anti-union laws the country has ever seen.

The 1980 Employment Act reintroduced many of the restrictions of the scrapped Trades Dispute and Trade Union Act, outlawing secondary picketing and restricting the number of people who could be on a picket line. The 1982 Employment Act went even further, banning 'political strikes' and narrowing the grounds on which workers could take strike action. Unions also became liable for damages caused by industrial action, allowing the government to claim up to a quarter of a million pounds from unions who opted to strike. Despite historic action such as the Miners' Strike of 1984 and 1985 – which flouted many of Thatcher's new rules – union membership steadily fell throughout the 1980s and '90s as union power decreased and highly unionised industries such as steel, coal, printing and dockyards were dismantled.[12] Between 1980 and 1998, the percentage of UK employees in a trade union fell from 52 per cent to 30 per cent.[13]

No government since has overturned the crippling legislation overseen by Margaret Thatcher. While Tony Blair's New Labour put some focus on the rights of individual workers, through initiatives such as the national minimum wage and protections against unfair dismissal, it failed to restore any col-

11   https://ons.gov.uk/employmentandlabourmarket/peopleinwork/work placedisputesandworkingconditions/articles/labourdisputes/2018 (last accessed November 2020).

12   https://theguardian.com/news/datablog/2010/apr/30/union-membership-data (last accessed November 2020).

13   etheses.lse.ac.uk/852/1/Charlwood_anatomy_union_membership_decline.pdf (last accessed November 2020).

lective voice or power to the unions. In fact, as we will go on to explore, conditions have worsened still. The Trade Union Act of 2016, introduced under the Conservative and Liberal Democrat coalition, represented the biggest legal attack on unions since Thatcher's reforms. Among its crackdowns were stipulations that ballots must attract a 50 per cent turnout in order for their results to be legally valid, that 14 days' notice must be given before strike action, that agency staff can be brought in as cover for striking workers, and that all picket lines must be overseen by named supervisors.[14]

What is a union?

In order to best understand what unions are, sometimes it is useful to begin with what they are not. Too often we think of unions in the abstract, as entities separate from us as individual workers and separate from the workforce as a whole. When you think of a union, perhaps you picture a logo or a building, a branded pin badge or a tote bag. Maybe it's a general secretary or a picket line. But do you picture yourself and your co-workers?

To think of the union as a distinct, unknowable body that will step in when times get tough is to misunderstand its purpose and existence. No infrastructure, marketing, elected representative or strike means anything without the strength in numbers of a united workforce who have made a commitment to one another. We, standing together, have the power to influence what the union believes, how it behaves, if and when it acts, and whether it wins. A union is a dynamic, living, breathing pact that only exists as its members.

Unison, the largest union in the UK, defines the typical activities of a trade union as 'providing assistance and services to

14 http://legislation.gov.uk/ukpga/2016/15/contents/enacted (last accessed November 2020).

their members, collectively bargaining for better pay and conditions for all workers, working to improve the quality of public
services, political campaigning and industrial action.' The
former of these are the functions we tend to think of when we
picture trade unions: protests and negotiations over bread and
butter issues like pay, conditions, working hours, and health and
safety. Typically, unions will undertake these activities in recognised workplaces – that is, where a certain number of staff are
members of the union and the employer has agreed to negotiate
with the union in the process known as collective bargaining.
Recognised workplaces have traditionally been more prevalent
in the public sector, where terms and conditions have improved
and largely been sustained as a result, and union favourability
and membership numbers remain higher. As we will go on to
see, a union's commitment to representing *members* rather than
workers in general is both pragmatic – in terms of resource, time,
and obligations to paying members – and sometimes problem-
atic, creating a catch-22 where large swathes of unorganised
workers simply remain unprotected.

Unions and workers have also always made use of a number
of other tactics beyond simply the strikes and bargaining we
might typically associate with them. In one example, writes
academic Alan Bryman, cast members at Disneyland engaged
in acts of everyday resistance by working within their contracts
but refusing to smile, fastening the seatbelts of rude customers
too tightly, and operating water rides in a manner that ensured
those customers were drenched.[15] In the UK, the UCU is just one
union which has used 'work-to-rule' tactics to protest excessive
workloads, instructing members to work only within their contracted hours and to set out-of-office email responses from the
moment their work day finishes. And, as we will explore, grass-

---

15   Alan Bryman, *The Disneyization of Society* (London: SAGE Publications, 2004).

roots unions have recently made increasing use of direct action, in which members forego negotiation and compromise to instead protest publicly and directly, for example through occupations, protests outside the headquarters of bad employers, and other forms of civil disobedience.

Jane McAlevey, the veteran American organiser and author of numerous books on union strategy, draws a distinction between three traditional union functions: advocacy, mobilising, and organising.[16] Advocacy, where workers are spoken for in grievances and negotiated for by representatives, is the most superficial function, she posits; ordinary workers are hardly involved in the process at all. Mobilising refers to engaging already enthusiastic activists in a specific campaign, a project which brings together a greater number of ordinary workers but which does little to reach anybody new. For this reason, says McAlevey, it is 'deep organising' which unions should focus on and commit to: the work of recruiting new members and building a bigger and broader power base.

Far from soapboxes, megaphones and 'rousing their workmates to rebellion with a single fiery speech', writes American historian and activist Mike Davis in his book *Old Gods, New Enigmas: Marx's Lost Theory*, the rank-and-file organiser is 'more like a patient gardener', sowing the seeds, cultivating the sprouts, and laying the groundwork for unionism to bloom.[17] The work of an organiser is long and hard, and involves finding common ground with those who initially seem nothing like you. It means reaching out to people of different backgrounds and character, going beyond those who are politically engaged and with social and cultural capital to raise the voices of the

16 Jane McAlevey, *No Shortcuts* (New York, Oxford University Press, 2016).
17 Mike Davis, *Old Gods, New Enigmas: Marx's Lost Theory* (London & New York: Verso, 2020), p. 48.

quietest and most marginalised, providing resources and information that speak to them. It means laying the groundwork and building the relationships, so that when the moment is right the union is ready. This is the hardest but most essential work of the labour movement.

Strongly connected and complimentary to the work of deep organising is the advancement of political education and class consciousness – something The Plebs League, founded in 1909 at Ruskin College, Oxford, understood deeply. The college, established three years earlier, was part of a drive to extend Oxford University's education to working-class adults, but had increasingly become reliant on donations from noblemen and royalty. When a permanent committee containing university representatives was set up to supervise the College's syllabus, its trade unionist students hit back against what they saw as attempts to instil the curriculum with pro-establishment ideas and social control of the working class by the establishment. The Plebs League was formed in protest, and its members went on strike, eventually breaking away to form the Central Labour College.

The concept of class consciousness is attributed to Marx, although he never used the phrase. Rather, he described the process of workers coming to recognise capital as their shared enemy, leading to their perception of a working class with common interests. Class consciousness, then, is an understanding of one's social and economic position relative to others, and relative to the wider system of capital. Prior to developing it, according to Marxist theory, workers are instead manipulated into possessing false consciousness – an incorrect understanding of their social position as an individual issue unrelated to wider structures.[18]

---

18 Karl Marx, *Capital: A critique of political economy, Volume One* (London: Penguin Books, 1990).

Class consciousness is built into the foundations of the union movement, and is essential to the movement's survival and to any advancement of working-class interests. It's not necessarily the first thing that draws people to unions, but it can often be the thing that makes them stay: successful unions will have a strategy that includes retaining members who arrive with a grievance or looking for advice, and moving them through the work of collectivising and organising, building class consciousness in the process. This work takes many forms, not all of them structured or formal. Sometimes it's the conversations you have at a social event, or the training delivered to newly elected workplace reps, and sometimes it's discussing a motion at a branch meeting or specific workshops designed to build new activists. It might be listening to seasoned trade unionists reminiscing about the old days, or it might be a conversation over WhatsApp. One IWGB member even told me about the role a union book club had played in informing their political outlook. However a new generation choose to advance their class interests, unions are an invaluable training ground for young workers. In conversation with friends I've made through activism and organising, we have often described our political consciousness as a light switch you can't turn back off; a Pandora's Box of injustice and rage. Unions create working-class citizens who spend their whole lives no longer being satisfied with the status quo or blaming themselves for their fortunes, and that is a powerful force indeed.

Due to many factors which we will focus on in the next chapter, unions in the UK have found themselves operating in increasingly hostile and treacherous terrain over recent years. As a result, the priorities of many large and well-established unions have shifted to become more focussed on service provision – legal and career advice; campaign support for established branches; restaurant discounts – than the kind of deep organising McAlevey describes, or the kind of political education the Plebs League were committed to. Unions are left with a dilemma: to keep working only for existing members in established but shrinking sectors is to ignore the fertile but untapped ground in growing ones such as hospitality and care. But to commit their already very limited resources here is to take a shot in the dark and one that might not pay off immediately. It is essential, then, that we work to fight back against the forces which disempower unions so that they might return to the deep organising work and building of class consciousness vital for the advancement of the working class.

The 'new' working class?

While the exploitative model of capitalist work endures, the shape of that work – and, subsequently, of the working class as a whole – has changed through modern history in ways both subtle and profound, most notably in the post-World War II years. Arguably the most acute shift in Britain's labour market and economy occurred under Margaret Thatcher in the 1980s, when there was a concerted effort (only made possible by the weakening of unions) to dismantle manufacturing and industry in order to usher in the growth of a financialised service economy. The effects of deindustrialization were brutal and are still being felt today: unemployment on a massive scale; the hollowing out of entire communities; the fall of families into poverty almost overnight. And the demographic of the UK's workers changed too, with British male labourers at the sharp end of job losses and women and migrants entering the labour market on a mass scale.

While Thatcher's restructuring of the economy was a disaster for the working class and therefore British society as a whole, on its own terms it initially appeared a success. After decades of cyclical boom and bust in the economy, the period between the early 1990s and 2008 saw sectors such as finance and higher education grow exponentially, bringing with them a booming and prosperous economy. But the boom was unsustainable and the bust dramatic; in 2008, the financial crash once again highlighted the volatile nature of an economy built on speculation, risk, and the concentrated power of a few bosses in the City of London. Unemployment was rife, austerity was to follow shortly, and people across the country were forced to reskill or claim benefits, upending the labour market once again.

Today, our labour market is dominated at the bottom end by women and migrants, and comprised mainly of sectors such as service and care, the successes of which are largely built on the exploitation of undervalued and unorganised workers. The days of unionised and secure jobs in manufacturing and industry, and a time when class was widely recognised as an organising principle for society, have long made way for precarious and exploitative work and an active attempt to obscure the experience and effects of class difference. As a result of these rapid changes and active political obfuscation, we are confused. Regular debates about what constitutes the working class play out on the pages of newspapers and in the tweets of activists, politicians and journalists. Class has come to encompass not only your relationship to waged labour, but various cultural and aesthetic markers, obscuring the role of the state and capital. Did you visit museums as a child? Have you ever eaten fish fingers for dinner? What kind of wallpaper did you have in your house growing up?

Perhaps the most recent development which has forced us to reckon with these categories is the Coronavirus pandemic. When the country became subject to nationwide lockdowns, it seemed that new classes of 'worker' were created overnight. We clapped for carers and other essential workers who put their lives on the line. We laughed when children and animals blundered into our colleagues' Zoom screens, making visible the usually hidden care and domestic work of the home. We cried when we read about Belly Mujinga, a Black train station worker who died with the virus after being spat at on the job,[19] one of thousands of Brits of colour who were disproportionately affected by the outbreak and disproportionately likely to work in front-line jobs. It was no longer clear-cut whose work was hardest or most demanding, or what the average working-class citizen looked like, but one thing was obvious: your work dictated how easy it was for you to protect yourself and your family from the virus, how insulated you were from the economic turmoil it unleashed, and how much freedom you were able to access through technology, second homes and car ownership, while many felt four walls closing in on them.

Today's UK, then, is a country where a manual labourer might easily earn more in a month than a teaching assistant at a university; where a Black woman going to work in a London train station might as well be heading down a mine. A salesman with no formal education could likely out-earn a graduate with three degrees entering the labour market into a recession and following a pandemic. A care home can be as treacherous a workplace as a factory line, and a call centre as precarious as a building site. The Coronavirus showed the public that the old categories don't apply anymore, and that there is little agreement about which do. Yet work still defines our lives, our health, our safety, our security and our future. Our relationship to it must be considered a central tenet of our class.

---

19   https://bbc.co.uk/news/uk-england-london-52938155 (last accessed November 2020).

Who needs unions?

Do you rely on work to survive? If so, you need a union. If you're not a boss, you need a union. Understandings of class remain contested and in flux, but there exists a widening gulf in experience between those whose survival depends on work and social security, and those whose prosperity is guaranteed by assets and inheritance. While the latter are insulated from economic hardship and emergency by their wealth, the former – the vast majority of us – need unions in order to have any hope of comparable protection, regardless of what our specific experience of work looks like day-to-day. Those in white-collar or secure and comfortable jobs where they feel happy and well-protected can be reticent about union membership, believing it to be for a different kind of worker. But unions are about strength in numbers, and your membership is an act of solidarity. And besides, the security and comfort enjoyed in these roles, from generous holiday allowances to sick pay and secure contracts, was more often than not secured by a strong union in the first place. Undoubtedly, different workers exist in entirely different conditions, face different challenges, and occupy different terrain. Our organising must be cognisant of this; one size will never fit all and union strategies must be attuned to these differences. But to be distracted by constructing distinct classes of worker in opposition to one another is to gloss over the huge, omnipresent truth that unites us: almost all of us have to sell the products of our labour to survive.

Unions also perform another role, and one which can be an important tool in any trade unionist's arsenal: they have a function within capitalism. Bargaining power is a key mediating force for keeping capital in check, ensuring it runs smoothly to the benefit of all participants; in essence, saving capitalism, a system built to escalate unconstrained, from itself. This might make would-be trade unionists uneasy, many of whom are likely to correctly identify capitalism as the source of our oppression and argue instead for a society organised by socialist, communist or anarchist principles. But as anti-capitalists existing within capitalism, there will always be a tension between how things are and how we wish they were. It is vital that we work to improve material conditions today, within the constraints of capitalism, while working towards a radically different future in the long-term. In fact, the former is an essential foundation for the latter.

For a while in the 2010s, it felt like the left could win state power in the West. Bernie Sanders in the USA, Jeremy Corbyn in the UK, Jean-Luc Melenchon in France, Alexis Tsipras in Greece and Pablo Iglesias in Spain all galvanised widespread public support and inspired rousing grassroots movements behind them. Many of these, including in the UK, were spearheaded and backed up by young activists and organisers, those of us who have grown up in the shadow of the financial crash and know nothing other than the failure of market capitalism and the total collapse and insidious erosion of institutions from banks to police forces to parliamentary democracies and the NHS. Today's young voters came of age through Occupy, the anti-war movement, student fees protests, climate strikes and, now, a global pandemic. We are politicised, angry, and willing to take to both the streets and the ballot box in pursuit of a better future.

But despite huge support and turnout among young voters in the UK, Jeremy Corbyn's Labour Party still lost in both 2017 and 2019, with the latter such a dramatic defeat that it marked the end of 'Corbynism' within the party and a return to the old politics of New Labour with the election of Keir Starmer as party leader. The status quo prevailed again; parliamentary politics let the young left down again. We didn't win state power in the

2010s, but we built networks, organised communities, articulated ideas, and envisioned a future which put people over profit and gave ordinary citizens control over their lives. If the ballot box wasn't the place for that vision, perhaps the picket line is. Electoral power is one important tool, but it means little without grassroots collectivism and durable working-class institutions that can survive changes in government. Power is never given freely; everyday people pledging their solidarity to each other and acting as one is the only thing that has ever changed working-class people's lives for the better.

Unions are not just mechanisms for protecting your rights at work, but vehicles for shaping society. Crucially, their work can scale up or down; communities and workplaces can be sites of resistance, solidarity and progress, alongside national and even global campaigning and camaraderie. Just as they balance workplace power, unions at large can also provide a counter to elites and corporations with disproportionate political and societal influence. And their impact is clear: numerous studies have linked the weakening of trade unions to the deepening of inequalities,[20] with unions increasing wages for the poorest 35 per cent and decreasing them for the top 20 per cent in a straightforward redistribution of economic power.[21]

As spaces of left organising and thought, then, unions are indispensable. Existing workers' rights are both insufficient and poorly enforced, and a functioning union movement must never lose sight of the need to fight both those battles. But state power has never been a neutral arbiter, and rights, though hard-won, are an insufficient framework for radical politics. As we rebuild

---

20   https://theguardian.com/inequality/2018/jun/10/rising-inequality-falling-union-membership (last accessed November 2020).

21   https://link.springer.com/article/10.1007/s12122-004-1011-z#page-1 (last accessed November 2020).

from electoral defeat, we should commit to building a base, articulating a vision, and the deep organising work of recruiting others to our cause and forging a new class consciousness. The strategies and methods of trade unionism provide us with an invaluable toolkit for this project, equipping us with ways of mapping power, understanding structures and building resistance from the ground up.

A union, then, is solidarity. It is representation, protection, advocacy. It is higher wages, equal pay, health and safety, and sick leave. It is mobilising and organising. It is picket lines and negotiations and marches and meetings. It is thinking and talking and building and planning. It is hope and optimism, fury and justice. It is as strong as its members and as weak as its members. It is a bond between people with shared interests and a commitment to one another. It is strength in numbers and power beyond parliament. It is reclaiming control over your life and taking a stand against the elites. It is base-building, ideology-forming, class-consciousness-raising. It is local and national and global. It is you and me and the millions of others beside us who can see a better future and are ready to forge it. A union is the workers and the workers are the union

Chapter 2

Your union isn't rubbish, it's disempowered

One of the most common responses I hear from politically engaged young workers who aren't members of or involved in their union is some variation of 'it's because my union is rubbish'. Mostly this group is comprised of young people who are sympathetic to the aims of unions, nominally on the left and aware on some level of the unjust nature of work and capitalism. Perhaps some might even grudgingly pay for a union membership out of a sense of obligation, but don't engage beyond that. Others among them express something akin to exasperation; a suggestion that they would love nothing more than to sign up, but there's simply nothing there for them. As one communications officer in the public sector put it to me, 'I'd join in a second if my union was any good, but I can't name one thing they've done.'

On some level, this analysis is understandable: we live in a capitalist system which has trained us to see through the eyes of the market, interrogating the value in everything we pay for and viewing those purchases solely as one-way services in the pursuit of acquisition. By these measures, paying your union dues could feel like throwing your hard-earned money away, rather than buying you anything immediately tangible. This objection, though, is one which fundamentally misunderstands both the very nature of the union, and the conditions in which it operates today. For a start, the weakness people perceive in their unions – real or imagined – is the intended result of decades of concerted erosion by governments and bosses. And crucially, our union membership isn't a subscription service we pay for but a gateway into a dynamic and active movement that we can and should help to build and reinvigorate. In other words, your union isn't rubbish, it's disempowered – and the only way to build back its power is by getting active.

Anti-union laws in practice

Undoubtedly the most profound way in which unions find their work frustrated is through draconian anti-union laws, which have served to intentionally and systematically dismantle collective power through the decades. As outlined in the previous chapter, these laws take many forms and have been introduced and welcomed by many governments. While Thatcher is widely identified as the prime minister who really smashed the unions, few before her made many efforts to structurally empower them and none since have sought to repeal the blockades she placed in their way. The 2016 Trade Union Act was second in the scale of its assault only to Thatcher's suite of attacks, and continues to obstruct union activities today. Josephine Grahl, Young Members' Officer at Unison, describes how anti-union legislation operates to disempower unions like hers:

I think the trade union laws are deeply restrictive and they need to be changed, but there's so many different aspects to that. Obviously the restrictions in the 2016 Trade Union Act are a big issue for Unison because they make it so much harder to have a strike ballot nationally and our major employers – the NHS and local government structures – are national structures. So we are basically in a situation where it's very difficult to be able to run a national ballot for strike action because of the 50 per cent threshold [required for a ballot to be legally valid]. But even before that, unions don't have the simple right to go into workplaces and organise there. An automatic right for unions to go into workplaces, even where there are hostile employers, and publicise the union and organise those workers would be a big step forward.

Anti-union laws come in many guises, from blatant restrictions on union activity through to the imposition of extensive bureaucracy designed to impede, complicate and delay industrial action. To outline each law and the ways it has served to weaken the movement would be to write an entire book in itself. But, as alluded to by Grahl and in the famous trade union proverb that 'collective bargaining without the right to strike is little more than collective begging',[1] examining how the right to strike specifically has been challenged throughout the years serves as a useful bellwether as to union power and government drives to limit it.

In 1980, the Employment Act limited picket line numbers and solidarity actions, as well as introducing public funds for unions to run ballots, essentially incentivising them to instigate bureaucracy which would ultimately hamper their activities, while also thwarting resistance by providing funding from the public purse. Once this door was open, an onslaught ensued. The 1982 Employment Act included penalties for officials who endorsed a strike without a ballot and the 1984 Trade Union Act widened

---

1   The origins of this phrase, widely quoted throughout the union movement, are unknown, although it is considered to have been popularised in a 1944 *Time* magazine article which quoted a union member opposed to no-strike agreements in place during wartime.

these penalties to cover any action at all taken without a ballot, as well as forcing unions to carry out ballots in secret and with specific wording on the ballot paper. By 1993, the cumulative effects of further laws on balloting included a requirement for unions to give notice of a ballot, to disclose to bosses the names of those balloted, and to conduct all ballots by post. To rupture collective strength, ballots were required to be held at individual workplaces rather than across entire workforces. To challenge any residual collective strength, they were also required to be independently scrutinised. Cumulatively, balloting legislation introduced government interference in the guise of regulation, paring back union independence through the exercise of state power.[2]

And while, legally, individual workers cannot be discriminated against for union membership, in practice they still are. In November 2020, for example, the UCU began balloting for strike action at the University of East London when active union members appeared to be targeted with threatened redundancies.[3] The UK is sometimes considered to be more amenable to trade unions when compared to the US, where access to healthcare is often contingent on union membership and recognition is therefore expensive for businesses. In response, a whole industry of anti-union law firms and consultancies has emerged.[4] But while the particular shape of union-busting varies, at its root is a truth that is shared on both sides of the Atlantic: businesses rely on the exploitation of their workers for

2   https://rmtlondoncalling.org.uk/content/briefing-anti-union-laws (last accessed April 2021).

3   https://newhamrecorder.co.uk/news/education/ucu-members-stike-over-uel-redundancies-7565970 (last accessed April 2021).

4   https://theconversation.com/the-labor-busting-law-firms-and-consultants-that-keep-google-amazon-and-other-workplaces-union-free-144254 (last accessed April 2021).

their survival and success. In the UK, legal protection for union members in practice is not a match for bosses determined to silence them.

Viewed in their entirety, the laws governing trade unions should be understood as existing solely to limit the power of workers to fight back. While individual members are theoretically protected as above, no collective protection for unions as entities exists in law. Each piece of legislation simply outlines limits on union activity; there are no corresponding protections, and no corresponding laws requiring employers or workplaces to, for example, ballot before changing contracts or make their finances available for inspection by employees. In fact, many pieces of trade union legislation go so far as to introduce further protections for employers against the 'threat' of unions.

The work of fighting back against anti-union laws is hard precisely because they exist. When unions were strong and united enough to resist an all-fronts assault, legislation had to be introduced slowly and carefully. That legislation – and the weakening of union democracy it sowed – disempowered the movement enough to make it vulnerable to more sweeping attacks. Now that unions find themselves with limited power and no protection, it's little surprise that the bold organising and big wins required to attract new members are fewer and further between.

A hostile political landscape

Explicit anti-union laws are just one part of the puzzle, however. While they single-handedly go some way to removing the teeth from unions and leaving workers unprotected, they also sit amid a wider political landscape which works alongside them to weaken the rights of workers and limit collective action. Since

Thatcher's premiership, successive governments have picked up the baton on policy which prioritises bosses, disempowers workers, and individualises rights while simultaneously dismantling any support for realising them. As we've explored, the structure of the UK's economy has changed dramatically in this time, with heavy industry waning, financial services booming, and sectors such as hospitality and care today making up the majority of the economy. It is important to understand this not as an inevitable process but as a concerted effort by Thatcher and subsequent leaders, exercised through tax changes, deregulation, privatisation, and the wilful weakening of trade unions. The fate of the UK labour movement has never been accidental or subject to organic and unstoppable forces, but rather dictated by powerful people on a mission to undermine it.

The gradual erosion of collective power in the UK has taken place against a backdrop of globalisation and financialisation, two connected forces which present both opportunities and threats for workers and the labour movement. Globalisation, the process by which the world has become increasingly connected and interdependent, has increased competition in the labour market and muddied the waters of regulation and enforcement, but also presents an opportunity for solidarity and resistance across borders. Financialisation, in which financial institutions take on ever-greater influence in an economy, erodes solidarity and strengthens capital at the expense of labour, but also makes plain structures of oppression and highlights a clear set of issues around which workers can organise. The opportunities exist, but the threats have so far won out and contributed to the consistent grinding down of working-class power.

At the root of much western political thought and action since the 1980s is neoliberalism, defined by writer David Harvey as 'a theory of political economic practices that proposes that human well-being can best be advanced by liberating individual entre-preneurial freedoms and skills within an institutional framework characterized by strong private property rights, free markets and free trade.'[5] As well as entrenching inequalities by rendering structural power invisible, neoliberalism's focus on individuals has had both an explicit and an insidious effect on the ability of unions to carry out the most basic of their functions. For the rich and powerful, the social principles of neoliberalism – indi-vidualism and entrepreneurship – collaborate with its economic principles of deregulation and austerity to concentrate wealth and consolidate power. When companies rake in profits and CEOs make their millions, we are told it is a sign of a thriving economic system, despite the inequalities that deepen as a result and the endless cycle of financial crashes and slow recovery that suggest otherwise.

But for the working class, those principles are designed to collide to devastating effect. For example, the erosion of col-lective rights in tandem with decreased public spending and privatisation has resulted in the individualisation of rights alongside the cutting of any support for enforcing them. With no right for third parties to take action on behalf of others, and no recourse for collective legal action against an employer, for example, individual workers are left to rely on an expensive and alienating maze of courts and tribunals, and instructed to seek guidance from services such as Citizens Advice Bureaux (CABx) should they need it. Since 2013, half of all CABx and legal advice centres in England and Wales have closed,[6] in large part due to cuts to legal aid which impeded access to justice from that year

5   David Harvey, *A Brief History of Neoliberalism* (Oxford University Press, 2005), p. 2.

6   https://theguardian.com/law/2019/jul/15/legal-advice-centres-in-england-and-wales-halved-since-2013-14 (last accessed November 2020).

on. Collective rights have made way for individual ones, but the pursuit of justice through individual means has become virtually impossible for most individuals who need to pursue it. This was highlighted once more in 2020 when Prime Minister Boris Johnson announced a return to workplaces following nation-wide lockdowns in the middle of the Coronavirus pandemic. In July that year, Johnson changed guidance on working from home to encourage office staff back to their desks in the same month that over 1,500 people in the UK died with the virus.[7] When challenged over the decision, he suggested that workers should make their own choices about their health and safety, and individually negotiate with bosses for a safe return to work.

Neoliberal ideals have also underpinned any supposed attempts by governments to tackle poor working conditions explicitly. When Matthew Taylor, Chief Executive of the Royal Society of the Arts and Head of Policy in Tony Blair's government, was appointed by Theresa May to chair a watershed 'review of modern employment' in 2016, it was a clear signifier of the government's approach to unions and the exploitation of precarious workers. Anyone confused by May's appointment of an opposition insider needn't have worried; Blair famously boasted about Britain's anti-union laws being the toughest in Europe, and his position of doing nothing at all to empower unions while emphasising individualism over collectivism paved the way for successive Conservative governments' positions of doing exactly the same.

The Taylor Review, officially titled *Good Work: the Taylor Review of Modern Working Practices*,[8] continued in this tradition.

---

7 https://Coronavirus.data.gov.uk/deaths (last accessed November 2020).

8 https://assets.publishing.service.gov.uk/government/uploads/system/uploads/attachment_data/file/627671/good-work-taylor-review-modern-working-practices-rg.pdf (last accessed November 2020).

Its panel, which included a corporate employment lawyer, a Deliveroo investor[9] and no trade union or worker representation, produced a report which the Independent Workers of Great Britain (IWGB) union described as 'replete with legal errors' and 'recommendations . . . so wishy-washy, it would be entirely feasible for government to "implement" them without any discernible impact on the workers they are designed to help, and certainly without any concrete improvement in workers' lives.'[10]

Class war?

Nobody does class solidarity like the rich. In May 2020, Baroness Dido Harding, a Conservative peer and wife of Conservative MP John Penrose, was appointed to lead the UK's privatised Coronavirus Test and Trace system, a programme later described by doctors as 'an utter shambles'.[11] Four months later, she was made interim chief of the National Institute for Health Protection, a body designed by management consulting firm McKinsey to replace Public Health England. The National Institute for Health Protection is overseen by a board including executives from the likes of Waitrose, Jaguar and TalkTalk – the latter of which Harding was previously chief executive, overseeing a period in which over 150,000 customers found their personal data stolen in a data breach.

Harding had never been through a standard recruitment process when she was appointed by the government. Nor had Topshop boss Sir Philip Green when he was selected as David

9   https://ft.com/content/95392a68-6596-11e7-8526-7b38dcaef614?mhq5j=e1 (last accessed November 2020).

10 https://theguardian.com/commentisfree/2017/jul/18/taylor-review-gig-economy-workers (last accessed November 2020).

11 https://theguardian.com/world/2020/sep/14/utter-shambles-gps-and-medics-decry-nhs-test-and-trace-system (last accessed November 2020).

Cameron's efficiency tsar in 2010, or venture capitalist Adrian Beecroft when he was commissioned in 2012 to provide a review of employment law, in which he suggested that workers might like to trade in their rights for business shares.[12] Nor, for that matter, had Matthew Taylor (CBE) of the Taylor Review. Property developer Richard Desmond also faced no such inconvenience in 2020 when he was allegedly able to influence planning decisions by being rich enough to make a £12,000 donation to the Tory party.[13] No amount of incompetence or negligence is a match for solidarity within the upper echelons of power. Money and influence speak louder than science, evidence, compassion or common sense.

'Class war' is an accusation levelled only at the working class (most notably when they attempt to highlight the unjust divisions within society), despite the boss class being better organised and far more militant than many trade unions or left-wing campaigns. In 2009, the UK Information Commissioner, the body responsible for upholding information rights, found that more than 40 major British companies had come together to fund a secret organisation with the intention of buying personal data to vet would-be employees and potentially blacklist 'troublesome' workers.[14] A decade later, the publication of police documents spelled out how the Metropolitan Police's Special Branch had backed up that operation with state power.[15]

---

12   https://gov.uk/government/publications/employment-law-review-report-beecroft (last accessed November 2020).

13   https://independent.co.uk/news/uk/politics/robert-jenrick-richard-desmond-property-development-tory-donor-cash-favours-a9568496.html (last accessed November 2020).

14   https://theguardian.com/uk/2009/mar/06/data-protection-construction-industry (last accessed November 2020).

15   https://bbc.co.uk/news/uk-47457330 (last accessed November 2020).

Today, high profile bosses like Lord Alan Sugar of Amstrad, Tim Martin of Wetherspoons and Charlie Mullins OBE of Pimlico Plumbers continue to moonlight as minor celebrities, media commentators and talking heads, advancing anti-worker rhetoric and action in both the public imagination and the halls of power. Employer bodies such as the Confederation of British Industry (CBI) and the Federation of Small Business (FSB), lobbying groups regularly invited to meet with government and influence policy, are viewed largely as neutral and measured actors within public life, while unions are painted as fringe organisations full of extremists. It is a fact of our organising that those interested in maintaining the status quo will always be seen as apolitical and objective and those interested in deconstructing it as partisan and biased.

Catch-22

These hostile conditions have created something of a vicious cycle for unions. The only way to resist and oppose them is, as with all trade unionism, through strength in numbers and deep organising. But the conditions themselves have an enduring impact on perceptions of unions, dissuading new members from joining, and rendering unions so weak as to be invisible. Research published by the TUC in 2020 sought to explore exactly these issues. The authors of *The Missing Half Million*[16] used WhatsApp diaries and interviews to investigate barriers to young workers' trade union participation, ultimately identifying four key challenges: low expectations of work to begin with; a lack of trust between colleagues; a sense of futility; and, crucially, a lack of

16 https://tuc.org.uk/sites/default/files/2020-01/WorkSmart_Innovation_Project_Report_2019_AW_Digital.pdf (last accessed November 2020).

knowledge about unions. Clare Coatman, a senior campaigner at the TUC who led the research, described this last finding:

> When we asked our hundred participants 'what do you think a trade union is?', the vast majority said: 'I don't know, I've never even heard those words,' which is a bit chilling. Where there was knowledge it either came from family members or it came from the media – they would talk about train drivers going on strike and so on. On the whole there were really warm associations with trade unions; if we give them a definition, they think it's a great idea. They'd say heartbreaking things like 'if only there was a union I was eligible to join as a care worker', and you're bursting to say: 'there is, there are several,' but because it's research you can't.

If young would-be organisers and activists are learning about unions from the media and their families, we have at best one more generation to turn things around. Declining membership numbers and influence mean the offspring of millennials and Generation Z are unlikely to learn about working-class solidarity from their parents, and the subsequent culling of industrial correspondents from major newspapers means union work is rarely covered beyond large-scale industrial action, controversy, or Labour Party infighting. While the British Army freely recruits in schools, trade union activity rarely appears on the curriculum and constitutes the type of political education which is subject to regular sensationalisation in media reports and censure by government ministers.[17]

It would be a mistake to think that the answer to problems like those identified by the TUC lies in slick marketing or increased

---

17 https://theguardian.com/world/2020/oct/20/teaching-white-privilege-is-a-fact-breaks-the-law-minister-says (last accessed November 2020).

membership perks. Young people's work lives are getting harder, and the imperative for collective responses is as strong as ever. Visible wins and material improvements will build and sustain a new generation of trade unionists, but these are ever harder to come by under the conditions outlined above. Unions must keep working for them, while never losing sight of the fight against the wider forces that undermine their work. Our demands must be as bold and uncompromising as the attacks bombarding us are.

The playing field upon which unions operate, then, is far from even. To acknowledge this is not to let the labour movement off the hook for the many ways in which it could and should evolve and improve – many of which we'll go on to explore in this book – but rather to map our organising conditions as they exist, and to identify the barriers we must dismantle and the arguments we must win. Whether it's opposing draconian anti-union legislation or resisting the institutionalisation of individualism, unions must bring what residual power they have to bear against the adversaries of the working class in order to one day build back more of it.

Chapter 3

Resisting the gig economy

Precarious work is nothing new – just ask care workers. Every Monday, 23-year-old Amy Saleem,[1] a care assistant with a private company in England, receives her timesheet for the following week. With no guaranteed hours, her shifts can vary drastically from week to week and often change – for better or worse – at the last minute. Technically an employee, she is entitled to holiday and sick pay, but to claim it means handing in a paper form to her company's headquarters several miles from her home, in her own unpaid time. Despite her role requiring her to move between different client's homes throughout the day, Saleem is paid only for time spent in their homes and not for travelling. 'When I'm at work I'm not always earning enough to live on,' she tells me. 'And when I'm not at work, I feel like I am anyway because my boss can phone at any moment.'

Workers like Saleem and others in the care sector – as well as cleaners, couriers, drivers and many more – have long experienced precarity of the type that has recently been brought to our attention by the 'gig economy', a modern sounding name for an age-old model of capitalist work which causes hardship and distress for far more than it benefits with its promise of flexibility and freedom. While insecure work seemed to emerge as

---

1   Not her real last name.

a cause for concern with the boom in app-based businesses, the 'gig economy' in reality marks an expansion of forms of exploitative employment which have always existed but which have traditionally been racialised and gendered, and therefore less visible. Despite its image today of young male students on bikes, this insecurity has long predominantly affected women and migrants. Women are more likely to seek out flexibility in the absence of affordable and accessible childcare. Migrants are often excluded from the traditional labour market and reliant upon employment that undercuts wages and denies the worker any benefits.

There is no agreed legal definition of 'precarious work' and governments have worked hard to obscure what it really means, framing precarious workers as innately vulnerable rather than acknowledging that it is their material conditions which make them so. Generally, it has come to be widely understood as work which is unstable, insecure, unprotected and poorly paid, often but not always on zero-hour contracts. In the UK, this encompasses the booming gig economy – dominated by newer companies like Deliveroo and Uber who have historically classed those who work for them as self-employed contractors rather than workers, thus sidestepping any obligation to obey employment law – as well as the increasing use of casual, freelance and temporary contracts in place of secure and permanent contracted work, a trend that has occurred in workplaces as wide-ranging as charities, start-ups, restaurants, hospitals and universities.

The text at the top of Deliveroo's rider application page reads 'Find work that suits you.' 'Make money on your schedule,' says the same page on Uber's website. On the sign-up page for Task-Rabbit, an app through which people can book assistance with tasks such as DIY and cleaning, are the words 'flexible work, at your fingertips.' Gig economy work is consistently sold to its workers as flexible, innovative and liberating, as if the work can be magically separated from its exploitative nature and the fact that the business models of these companies essentially rely on employing people without giving them employment rights. Behind the jargon and these attempts to reframe precarious work as something exciting and freeing, casualisation and the proliferation of zero-hour contracts and other forms of insecure employment have led to very real harms. As Amy Saleem describes, workers are constantly at the whim of their bosses, unable to plan ahead either in terms of schedule or income, and not always able to take on a second job when they need to be able to drop everything if their first calls them up. With no guarantee of hours, many insecure workers find themselves in poverty despite being in work, and report anxiety and other mental health problems as a result of their precarity.[2] A perfect storm of factors come together to make this group of workers uniquely vulnerable: they disproportionately represent the demographics least likely to be trade union members – migrants, young workers, the low-paid – and occupy sectors like hospitality, retail and care where bullying, harassment and discrimination is high and union membership is low. Their bosses don't care about them, the government won't protect them, and in many cases unions aren't fighting for them either, focussing resources instead on existing members and a strategy built for the manufacturing economy of the twentieth century and not the service economy the UK has long since shifted to. But as we'll see, victories for the UK's precarious workers are there for the taking if only unions can be bold enough to try and win them.

---

2   https://tuc.org.uk/sites/default/files/insecure work report final final.pdf (last accessed November 2020).

Precarious work in numbers

One of the difficulties in organising precarious workers is their relative invisibility. Those working cash in hand leave no trace on employment or tax statistics and anyone looking at the numbers of self-employed people in the UK has no way of knowing how many of those would rather be on a secure contract or are being exploited in what is termed 'bogus self-employment'. With no agreed definition of precarious work, the Office for National Statistics (ONS) doesn't publish a figure for those undertaking it. The ONS does, however, collect data on zero-hour contracts, and this shows a sharp rise in their use since 2009; in February 2020,[3] the number of people on zero-hour contracts in the UK was 974,000, an all-time high and more than double that a decade prior. The most recent attempt at documenting the numbers of precarious workers in the UK was undertaken by the TUC in 2019.[4] Their research, which defined precarious workers as the low-paid self-employed, agency and casual workers without fixed-term contracts, and those on zero-hour contracts, suggested 3.7 million workers – that's one in nine workers – could be classed as precarious.

Undoubtedly a small number of these workers would say that they are happy with their work arrangement, but research undertaken by the Union of Shop, Distributive and Allied Workers (USDAW) in 2017[5] also tells another story. One in three respondents to the survey were in what the union termed

---

3   https://ons.gov.uk/employmentandlabourmarket/peopleinwork/employment andemployeetypes/datasets/emp17peopleinemploymentonzerohourscontracts (last accessed November 2020).

4   https://tuc.org.uk/research-analysis/reports/insecure-work?page=0 (last accessed November 2020).

5   www.usdaw.org.uk/CMSPages/GetFile.aspx?guid=d0996e4e-af69-4efa-8743-a804b2426c0a (last accessed November 2020).

'underemployment'. That is, working fewer hours than they wanted or needed to. Almost 30 per cent of respondents either had or were looking for a second job. That this was the norm among retail, warehouse and distribution workers points again to a proliferation of insecurity in traditional sectors, and not just within start-ups and young businesses like Deliveroo and Uber. In other words, even unions which remain insistent on strategising only for their existing membership will find that precarious work is very much their problem too.

The boom described above cannot be divorced from the weakening of trade unions over the same time period, as we've already explored. But alongside the purposeful erosion of collective and working-class power, a range of other related factors have worked together to introduce precarity to the UK labour market in profound ways. Some are ideological. Neoliberalism saw ideas about business efficiency seep into the public consciousness like never before. High on the political agenda was the 'cutting of red tape', code for a shift in the risk attached to paid work onto workers and away from employers. In the Blair years, an emphasis on 'employability' in practice saw employment framed as an individual responsibility while little was done to support it structurally. And looming large above all of this, neoliberalism's holy grail: the illusion of choice and endless freedom. Don't you want your work to be more flexible? Doesn't it make you feel powerful to be your own boss?

At the same time, outsourcing, extended by every government since Thatcher's, has seen bosses across the country reduce their employment responsibilities and cut their costs. The act of contracting another company to provide a function rather than doing so internally, outsourcing has spread across Britain's economy despite proving itself over and over to fail on almost every level. In 2012, the army were drafted in to provide security at London's Olympic Games after G4S, contracted to do so, failed to provide it.[6] Serco, which brazenly describes itself as 'shaping UK public services',[7] is contracted with the running of a number of state functions, including the notorious Yarl's Wood immigration detention centre where detainees have consistently alleged sexual abuse and violence, and inspections have found unsafe and unsanitary living conditions.[8] Outsourcing continually fails the public just as it fails its workers, with the latter finding themselves bearing the burden of this cost-cutting with worse terms than they would be on were they employed in-house. While not unique to young workers, the growth of outsourcing has a particular impact on those entering the job market onto new contracts, while long-standing employees remain on their original agreements. As well as being rife with precarious and insecure arrangements, outsourcing also hides a multitude of sins, not least that numerous different employers can operate under one roof, rendering any attempts at traditional organising or comparison of terms and conditions frustratingly difficult, if not impossible.

Precarity has also been able to flourish in the labour market where government and big business have been quick to cynically leverage progressive developments designed to benefit and empower workers. Measures such as flexible working are now the norm in many workplaces across the country, and were fought for by unions and equality campaigners alike. They were correct in arguing that these rights would give some control back to workers and have wide-ranging societal benefits,

6 https://theguardian.com/sport/2012/jul/12/london-2012-g4s-security-crisis (last accessed February 2021).

7 https://serco.com/about/our-strategy/shaping-uk-public-services (last accessed February 2021).

8 https://bbc.co.uk/news/uk-33043395 (last accessed February 2021).

including improving women's participation in the labour market by providing them with the means to better balance childcare and work. But increasingly often they are co-opted and manipulated into counterfeit flexible working measures like zero-hour contracts and bogus self-employment, in which the flexibility is in fact granted to the employers, at the expense of their workers. Similarly, many of the potential benefits of globalisation have been pounced on by the same powers, with bosses capitalising on what they see as an increasing pool of cheap and disposable migrant labour, a workforce that has been consistently demonised by right-wing media and politicians. Today, migrants are one of the groups most concentrated in precarious work and in some of the industries where it is most prevalent: caring, hospitality and manual labour.[9] And yet, many unions have struggled to effectively organise migrant workers, encountering challenges such as fears over immigration status, language barriers and a lack of knowledge about the UK's union structures.

That our apparent progress can so ruthlessly be capitalised on by our bosses presents a challenge in our fight against precarity, and for fair work more broadly. The Coronavirus pandemic, for example, opened up new conversations about many measures the left have long been calling for: remote working; a four-day week; universal and free internet access. But almost immediately these conversations were hijacked by capitalists who sought to discuss them in terms of productivity, monitoring and staff retention rather than liberation, equality and well-being. The labour movement must remain vigilant to these attempts to co-opt our demands, working to fight both against individual instances of precarity built on so-called freedom, and for a movement strong enough to resist this trend overall.

---

9 https://migrationobservatory.ox.ac.uk/resources/briefings/migrants-in-the-uk-labour-market-an-overview/ (last accessed February 2021).

A challenge and an opportunity

Precarious workers are difficult to organise precisely because they are precarious. Turnover is high and workers don't always have a particularly strong connection to the organisation, often being more likely to just move on than to try and improve things where they are. This also makes them easily replaceable, removing a lot of leverage: why should a boss cave to your demands when they can sack you instead and find someone else tomorrow? Why would you even make demands at all when your employment status is within their power?

The nature of precarious work also specifically undermines collectivism and solidarity. Workers are often in direct competition with each other for shifts, and in many cases don't even know or regularly see their colleagues. While traditional union organising models frequently talk about staff rooms and water cooler conversations, today's precarious workers book shifts through an app or have no physical headquarters. There's little incentive to collectivise, let alone much opportunity to do so. There are practical barriers, too, to organising this workforce. Shifts change at the last minute and there are families to support, second jobs to work, the daily grind to be endured before you even get to thinking about campaigning. The reasons these workers need unions are the same reasons unions can find them particularly difficult to reach or, depending on how you look at it, particularly easy to ignore.

But while these factors can make organising precarious workers a uniquely challenging undertaking, anyone concerned with membership numbers must also see their potential strengths. Workers with little loyalty to a company and embedded in a culture of fast turnover and multiple bosses might be convinced they have little to lose from organising. Where colleagues are competitors, they're also the people who cover your shift when you have a night out to go to, or who you have the best nights out *with,* precisely because you're all in the same precarious boat and feel each other's pain. And without any workers' rights, 'independent contractors' are not covered by authoritarian trade union laws and find a greater array of tactics available to them.

Research undertaken by the STUC in 2019[10] showed that while workers in hospitality and retail were more likely to identify as precarious workers, the term resonated less with those in agency work and bogus self-employment. Rather than labels, it was experience that united precarious workers of all stripes, most notably a lack of time, control and trust. Those involved reported feeling like they had little time to themselves to rest, socialise or think about things other than work, and spoke both of employers' control over them and a loss of control over their own lives as a result of insecure work. There was also a widespread sense that workers were often made to act in competition with one another or to reproduce existing hierarchies, sowing mistrust among colleagues. If unions can speak to young, insecure workers in these terms and prioritise everyday concerns over semantics, they may find they are knocking on an open door.

Getting organised

When Francis B. Scaife, a 24-year-old courier in Teesside, noticed in 2019 that their pay was delayed, they googled 'self-employed union'. Typical of lots of app-based work, Scaife is technically a contractor, self-employed but reliant on a single delivery

---

10   www.stuc.org.uk/files/Policy/Research-papers/precarityreport.pdf (last accessed November 2020).

boldly to call out bad bosses and authoritarian anti-union governments. The results have been a number of successes which punch above the weight of what are often small, overstretched, shoestring operations. Scaife's case is in many ways a perfect example of the dynamism and responsiveness that independent unions are capable of. When Scaife contacted the IWGB, the union didn't have any courier members where they lived and worked. Instead of turning them away, the IWGB voted within a month to accept members from outside London and establish a branch in the North East. Despite having no recognition with Scaife's employer, the union immediately took to Twitter, directing tweets at the company calling them out for poor practices and threatening to escalate if they didn't pay up. 'Within about a day we suddenly all got paid,' recalls Scaife.

Aside from assertive social media strategies, independent unions like IWGB and United Voices of the World (UVW) have also demonstrated their serious organising know-how. When UVW forced the London School of Economics to bring its mostly female, entirely migrant and BME cleaning workforce – many of whom had never been in a union before – back in-house in 2017, it represented one of the most significant trade union wins in the higher education sector for decades. To secure it, they made use of tactics as old as unions themselves: recruiting, balloting, striking and not giving in until their demands were met. And when sister union IWGB secured arguably its most high-profile victory, it made similar use of bread and butter trade union tactics. After organising Uber drivers in London under the banner of the United Private Hire Drivers branch, drivers backed by the union and by GMB took their fight to be recognised as workers rather than self-employed contractors to the courts, emerging victorious from Employment Tribunal, Employment Appeal Tribunal and the Appeal Court in turn. In

February 2021, the UK's Supreme Court ruled that Uber drivers should be classed as workers – not contractors – for the time they are logged into the app, in a move that will undoubtedly have ramifications across the entire gig economy.[11]

These unions have also taken seriously the challenge and urgency of unionising migrant workers, without whom little effective organising against precarious work is possible. This mission has sometimes meant revolutionising British union traditions. The IWGB's University of London branch, home to a large number of Latin American workers, bookends meetings with socialising where workers bring their families, share empanadas and beer, and dance to Latin American music, combining the enduring union values of solidarity and collective action with a new format which speaks directly to its members. Union materials are translated into multiple languages and caseworkers and organisers are recruited to work directly with specific migrant groups with whom they have a connection. This groundwork has paid off on multiple occasions, perhaps most notably through IWGB's '3 cosas' campaign at the University of London. Translated as 'three things,' a predominantly female and migrant outsourced workforce called for increased annual leave, enhanced sick pay, and adequate pension contributions. Over a number of years, these workers organised strikes, boycotts and protests, ultimately securing their demands in 2013[12] and then keeping up the fight; in 2020, the same workforce were finally brought in-house.[13]

11   https://theguardian.com/commentisfree/2021/feb/20/uber-ruling-government-workers-rights-conservatives-employers (last accessed February 2021).

12   https://independent.co.uk/student/news/victory-cleaning-staff-strike-university-london-wins-major-concessions-pay-and-conditions-8972785.html   (last accessed February 2021).

13   https://leftfootforward.org/2020/11/cleaners-at-london-universities-just-secured-victory-after-years-of-protest/ (last accessed February 2021).

Not every campaign has been won, yet, but many still highlight important lessons for organisers and the union movement more widely. UVW's 2020 attempt to use the 2010 Equality Act to argue against the outsourcing of security guards at St. George's University in London – on the basis that they were mostly migrants, and so their different treatment amounted to racial discrimination – highlighted a creative use of a different area of law, in the absence of strong employment rights.[14] An IWGB attempt to sue the government over a lack of protection for low-paid and precarious workers during the 2020 Coronavirus pandemic similarly illustrated a daring that larger counterparts could learn from. In their short lives so far, then, independent unions set up explicitly for precarious workers have shown how trade union models and structures can work just as effectively for this workforce if only the leap is taken to organise them in the first place. Flexibility within union structures has allowed them to be responsive to needs, while their small scale and political independence has gifted them the opportunity to take risks and think creatively about tactics.

A cross-union cause

In Scotland, the traditional union movement has been quick to get behind attempts to organise the nation's precarious workers. The Better than Zero campaign, set up in 2015, began as a campaign of all unions and none to organise workers in Scotland's hospitality sector, though it has since grown to encompass precarious workers of all kinds, while the Unite Hospitality campaign, which we will discuss in Chapter 9, remains focussed on the former. Initially made up of seasoned union organisers

---

14 https://uvwunion.org.uk/en/news/2020/07/legal-challenge-st-georges-institutional-racism/ (last accessed November 2020).

and a cohort of fed-up workers, the campaign quickly gained notoriety and won the backing of a number of unions and Scotland's Trade Union Congress, who continue to resource it today. 'Better than Zero has done well at punching above its weight,' says Tam Wilson, who oversees the campaign. 'Most young hospitality workers in Scotland know what it is – and all their employers definitely do.'

Better than Zero has become particularly well-known in Scotland's biggest cities Glasgow and Edinburgh, both of which boast a high number of student workers, for its direct campaign tactics and strong social media presence. Workers, whether union members or not, are encouraged to report their experiences on Facebook and Twitter, where staff and organisers (in reality just two people) can spot patterns and pick up on emerging issues, acting quickly to collectivise the issue and organise, and to call out employers publicly in the hope of shaming them into action. It was a combination of these methods that led to Better than Zero's earliest success, when the group forced the G1 behemoth, Scotland's largest hospitality employer, to standardise pay and scrap zero-hour contracts. The victory followed a sustained campaign that made use of direct actions like flash mobs and the stickering of menus and merchandise with Better than Zero's logo, as well as a victory at tribunal, arguably destroying G1's reputation to this day and firmly cementing their own. These days it's fair to say that many unscrupulous employers dread the Better Than Zero sticker treatment, while many shafted young workers will turn to the campaign ahead of a traditional union.

This was certainly the case when Better than Zero saw its work explode during the Coronavirus pandemic in 2020, when precarious workers across the country found themselves in limbo, ineligible for much government support and shunned by their employers. In one notable case, a group of beauty therapists at a

PURE Spa branch in the Silverburn Centre, Glasgow, reached out to Better than Zero about being forced onto zero-hour contracts while the salon was closed during the outbreak, essentially absolving their employer of any responsibility to keep paying them or to enrol them onto the government's furlough scheme. After being supported to join the GMB and winning their dispute to the tune of full pay and enrolment on the furlough scheme, they dubbed themselves the Silverburn Suffragettes.

'Better than Zero is more about offering tools and support for workers to campaign themselves, whether it's under our banner or their own, or the banner of a different union – it doesn't really matter to us,' says Tam Wilson, reflecting on what exactly has made Better than Zero so successful at organising precarious workers. 'We're not creating the issues or pushing people through a structure, we're just elevating their voices and providing a space for them to explore how they want to campaign. I think that's something the wider trade union movement could take on board.'

Where the campaign also diverges from large parts of the traditional movement is in a willingness both to speak and act plainly, tailoring language to workers unfamiliar with a union lexicon and being unafraid to make use of sabotage tactics the likes of which larger unions have tended to steer clear of in a move towards mediation and negotiation in place of direct action – an approach in which activists make use of their own power to directly achieve goals through protest and civil disobe-dience, rather than, for example, appealing to decision-makers or simply raising awareness. The Better than Zero approach hinges on the idea that such action is both valuable in and of itself, and the best recruiting tool there is. Rather than acting only for established members who need to wait a certain amount of time to become eligible for support, the campaign will respond immediately to urgent crises on the understanding that it is exactly this action which creates trade unionists and keeps them engaged. Once campaigns are won and contracts are reinstated, the workers who benefit are encouraged to stay involved, spread the word and build their power. It's not just a nice idea; the G1 action at Better than Zero's conception ultimately resulted in 300 new members.

A global fight

While many of the battles for precarious workers are won at a local level, be it London Uber drivers or the Silverburn Suffragettes, the fight against the exploitative gig economy is an international one. Many of the employers operating in these sectors are global enterprises or part of global supply chains – or even, to take Uber's case, some of the biggest private companies on the planet. Just a year after IWGB and GMB members launched their court action against Uber, a group of South African Uber drivers also won the right to be classified as employees following a court case in which the issues raised were very familiar: long working hours for low pay; the potential to be dismissed from the platform without notice at any given moment. Nicole Moore, a Lyft driver in California and organiser with Rideshare Drivers United, was one of hundreds of drivers from around the world who, in January 2020, attended the first ever meeting of the International Alliance of App-Based Transport Workers (IAATW) in Oxford organised by IWGB and others. 'What's amazing is we find so much commonality across all the countries,' she tells me.

Right now, companies across the world are doing exactly the same things to us all: depressing wages, working to get close to government and elected officials, trying to rewrite labour law. We're dealing with some of the largest international companies out there, so we have to be organising at an international level too.

Internationally and within the UK, the message is clear: precarious workers are ready and willing to fight back with or without the backing of the traditional labour movement – and it can only be in both parties' interests, and those of our changing workforce, to combine that power.

'I think the best role for organised labour is not to take over or co-opt it, but to add your strength to the fight that the drivers and workers are leading,' says Moore. 'The last vestiges of working-class resource and power are in the labour movement that is still standing, and we can help build its next era.'

Chapter 4

Beyond equality and diversity: The case for a liberatory unionism

When Jayaben Desai walked off her job at the Grunwick Film Processing Factory in London's Willesden in August 1976, she probably didn't know that she was to become something of a poster girl for discussions of equality and representation within the labour movement. Likely she was thinking of the long hours she'd worked over a record-hot summer, or the meagre wages she'd been paid in return, or the lack of respect she'd been treated with by managers who, among other impositions, required workers to ask permission before using the toilet.[1] Either way Desai walked off the job, setting in motion two years of strike action, a bitter split within the labour movement, and a contentious narrative of racial and gender equality as it applies to trade union history.

The Grunwick factory workers, mostly employed to manually develop other people's holiday photos, were mainly female and of South Asian origin. They primarily came from families who had settled in East Africa during colonial rule and who had subsequently been expelled after those countries gained

---

1   https://striking-women.org/module/striking-out/grunwick-dispute (last accessed November 2020).

independence from Britain. Bosses such as those at Grunwick capitalised on this new migrant workforce who they assumed to be submissive and willing to accept poor pay and conditions in their desperation for work. But those bosses were wrong. On Friday 20 August 1976, and despite not being members of a union, Desai led a group of workers out on strike in protest at their poor treatment by management. What began as a small-scale protest endured as seasons changed and both sides held out, but support for the Grunwick strikers grew with large marches across London and visits of solidarity from prominent trade unionists including Arthur Scargill of the National Union of Mineworkers.

The Grunwick Strike marked a historic moment in union history, so the narrative goes: migrant women taking action for themselves; a previously fractured, often racist and misogynistic trade union movement uniting behind them; an exercise in solidarity and union values. It was, after all, just eight years earlier that London's dockyard workers marched in support of Enoch Powell[2] and that the women of Dagenham's Ford factory had to overcome male hostility to strike for equal pay.[3] But it wasn't to last: after two years, under pressure from the government when the strikers rejected all attempts at compromise, the TUC withdrew support for the strike and left the Grunwick women out in the cold. Not even a hunger strike outside the TUC's head-quarters could regain their support. The women were forced to give up, with Desai commenting: 'Trade union support is like

2   https://workersliberty.org/story/2009/02/12/we-were-saying-%E2%80%94-1968-when-london-dockers-struck-work-and-marched-tory-racist-enoch (last accessed February 2021).

3   https://theguardian.com/politics/2013/jun/06/dagenham-sewing-machinists-strike (last accessed February 2021).

honey on the elbow: you can smell it, you can feel it, but you cannot taste it.'[4]

In Maya Goodfellow's book *Hostile Environment,* Dr Sunduri Anitha, whose work focusses on the Grunwick strike, calls this narrative into question. 'There were many other disputes where [South Asian women] were active before,' she says. 'They aren't in our consciousness because they weren't supported and therefore they failed . . . it's not an exception that they stood up to fight for their rights, they'd been doing it a long time before and they've done it for a long time since.' In response, Goodfellow writes:

> When people celebrate Grunwick as a rare moment of migrant resistance, or fetishise the women involved as 'strikers in saris', they reproduce the stereotype of Asian women as sub-missive, passive bystanders in history. But the UK's history of racist legislation and exploitative working conditions is, it should always be remembered, one of resistance.[5]

The story of the Grunwick strike teaches us three lessons: that despite stereotypes of male breadwinners, the most bold and effective action is often taken by the most marginalised workers; that solidarity has not always been extended as uncondition-ally to these workers as to their white male counterparts; and that narratives about these struggles are contested and often manipulated by those who would seek to undermine them. The latter of these is a dilemma the union movement continues to grapple with. On the one hand, very real issues exist and a great many brave and bold activists work tirelessly to highlight and

4 https://striking-women.org/module/striking-out/grunwick-dispute (last accessed November 2020).

5 Maya Goodfellow, *Hostile Environment* (London & New York: Verso, 2019) pp. 84–5.

challenge them. On the other, these struggles have often been capitalised on by those who care very little about liberatory politics but have a vested interest in discrediting trade unions. Their caricatures of smoke-filled rooms and gentlemen's agreements erase and undermine the brilliant organising work being done by women and other marginalised groups in arenas as diverse as fast food, outsourcing, cleaning, education and more. An already downtrodden and disempowered movement can be wary of challenging itself for fear of falling into this same trap or giving ammunition to its detractors. But it is vital that we do, for a movement that enshrines or perpetuates the very power relations that further marginalise workers is no movement at all.

As we will explore, today's unionism can be seen as being in something of a transition period between the outright hostility and division faced by marginalised workers in union spaces prior to Grunwick and after it, and a model of unionism that truly accounts for the ways in which our class and material circumstances are reinforced and reproduced through, for example, our gender, race, sexuality or disability. While we find ourselves in a time where most unions and many members would surely renounce the bigotry woven through labour history, many union leaders have not yet responded beyond equality and diversity initiatives and a focus on representation which, while often well-meaning, are incapable of bringing about the radical redistribution of power that marginalised workers need. When I call for a liberatory unionism, I refer to one that challenges this structure rather than working within its parameters; a unionism built on an understanding that women and disabled people suffer disproportionately at the hands of austerity[6] and that almost half of all trans people have had to leave their jobs

6   https://theguardian.com/society/2017/nov/17/women-and-disabled-austerity-report-tax-benefits-reforms (last accessed April 2021).

because they felt unwelcome.[7] That works to address the reality that Black women are twice as likely as their white counterparts to be in insecure work[8] and that the unemployment rate for young Black men is rising more sharply and faster than for any other group.[9] That takes as fundamental the truth that there can be no meaningful victories for the working class as a whole, as long as its most marginalised members are left on the sidelines. This path is not linear and its end point is not fixed. But until we move beyond the politics of representation and diversity to a model of liberatory unionism that understands and responds to the intersectional nature of these struggles, solidarity will continue to be extended conditionally to our most marginalised and our bosses will continue to divide and conquer.

The white male breadwinner model

Forty-two years on from the Grunwick strike, in October 2018, I watched in awe as 8,000 low-paid cleaners, cooks and care-workers filled up Glasgow's George Square at the culmination of a march through the city. The majority female workforce, employed by the city's council, were taking part in the UK's biggest equal pay strike since the introduction of the Equal Pay Act in 1970. As women hugged, cheered and danced to a playlist of feminist songs being blasted out into the crowd, I was struck again by what had been clear throughout their 12-year battle: beyond this square, nobody was really watching. Ahead of the strike I had written about this struggle for the *Guardian*,

---

7   https://theguardian.com/society/2021/mar/22/more-trans-people-hiding-identity-at-work-than-five-years-ago-report (last accessed April 2021).

8   https://tuc.org.uk/research-analysis/reports/bme-women-and-work (last accessed April 2021).

9   https://trustforlondon.org.uk/news/uk-youth-unemployment-rate-continues-rise-young-black-men-are-particularly-affected/ (last accessed April 2021).

comparing the women's plight to that of refuse workers in Birmingham who had rightfully received weeks of headline coverage for their industrial action a few years earlier, and the Hollywood actresses speaking out amid the #MeToo scandal, who had seen the full force of mainstream feminism leveraged behind them. Posing a question that I have since found quoted back to me and included in numerous accounts of the strike, I wrote: 'Could it be that Glasgow's equal pay women are too female to be a proper workers' rights story, and too working-class to be a proper feminist one?'[10]

The women of Glasgow and Grunwick knew that their poor treatment at work was fundamentally shaped by their gender and their race. But support fractured behind them, or failed to materialise, because the movement was not built to understand how. Since its formation, and despite continual challenges throughout its history, the labour movement's structures, strategies and priorities have been based on a model of a straight, white, non-disabled, British, male breadwinner as the default worker and citizen, because waged labour itself was largely built on the same model. If you've ever despaired at how a person might be expected to effectively juggle full-time work, hobbies, socialising, familial obligations and keeping a clean house, you're not alone. Traditional pay and shift structures were designed for male labourers on the assumption that their female partners would stay home, taking care of this domestic and emotional work for no remuneration and little recognition.

This segregation of roles, often referred to as the gendered division of labour, is built on the idea that the spheres of 'productive' labour primarily done by men and 'reproductive' labour primarily done by women map neatly onto 'work' and 'home'

---

10   https://theguardian.com/commentisfree/2018/sep/28/thousands-women-striking-solidarity-glasgow-pay (last accessed November 2020).

respectively. While there are myriad factors underpinning this division, the process of industrialisation both highlighted and institutionalised this separation and the concept of the nuclear family within capitalist relations. As waged labour undertaken by men became more structured and regimented, the unpaid role of women in the home was simultaneously cemented as essential in freeing up those same men to leave the house and earn what was seen as a 'family wage'. When women did undertake waged labour (as working-class women have always had to), it was often in the form of piecework done within the home and therefore still hidden and 'private', in comparison to men's public work. At the same time, bosses worked successfully to sow division between British and migrant workers, the latter of whom were constructed as a threat to the family wage and the family unit. The aim of regulation and of collective bargaining when it followed, then, was to ensure the standard British male worker a job that was full-time, permanent and unencumbered. In this way, we can see both how the unpaid labour of women – in maintaining a home and a family, as well as producing and nurturing the future workforce – is the bedrock of capitalism, and how the model of a straight, white, non-disabled British man as the ideal worker came to be formalised.

The breadwinner model has persisted and continues to shape our understanding of the archetypal worker and, by extension, the archetypal trade unionist. But it has not been without challenge. The Wages For Housework campaign which emerged from the women's movement in the 1970s called on its surface for women to be paid for this private, domestic work as men were for their public waged labour. But in her influential pamphlet *Wages Against Housework*, feminist organiser Silvia Federici wrote that to demand wages for housework does not mean to say that if we are paid we will continue to do it. It means precisely the opposite. To say that we want money for housework is the first step towards refusing to do it, because the demand for a wage makes our work visible.[11]

The demand was impossible; to pay women for their unpaid labour would require a radical restructuring of society and a radical redistribution of wealth. This impossibility was the point.

And just as the Wages For Housework campaign required women to self-organise autonomously from traditional union structures where their demands were largely unrecognised or unwelcome, a number of Black and migrant movements throughout the 1960s and 1970s also found their support in the wider community rather than the trade union movement. The first major strike by workers of colour in the UK took place at Courtald's Red Scar Mill in Preston, where West Indian workers were concentrated in particular production line roles. When managers tried to force these workers to cover more machines for less pay, they were supported by local union officials and white workers while Asian workers took strike action, backed by the Asian community locally.[12] While the labour movement was not universally hostile, it undoubtedly prioritised the interests of its white, male members at the expense of Black and migrant workers. In another example, an official from the Association of Scientific, Technical and Managerial Staff in Birmingham publicly denounced Enoch Powell after his infamous 'rivers of blood' speech, but was quickly contacted by a union member

---

11   Silvia Federici, *Wages Against Housework* (London: Power of Women Collective, 1975) p. 5.

12   http://unionhistory.info/britainatwork/narrativedisplay.php?type=raceand tradeunions (last accessed April 2021).

telling him to 'mind the union business', instead of looking after a group of people the member referred to by a racial slur.[13]

These attitudes still exist in parts of today's labour movement and society, and have even seen a resurgence as equality and diversity efforts have increased. Although not new, terms like 'white working class' have gained traction in recent years, serving at different turns as nostalgia, weapon, dog whistle, and obfuscation. The motives of its peddlers are clear: beneath the apparently benign, literal language, is a suggestion that white people (used interchangeably and incorrectly in this context with British men) have been disadvantaged by diversity and inclusion, that there is something unique about the experience of the *white* working class, and that this is a demographic which merits special treatment. To affix the word 'white' on the front of 'working class' is to posit that there is something distinct about the relationship between whiteness and class. And yet people of colour in the UK disproportionately live in poverty, most notably those of Black, Indian, Pakistani and Bangladeshi descent.[14] When the economy crashed in the 1970s, the number of unemployed Black and Asian workers rose by 290 per cent, nearly three times as fast as the jobless total as a whole.[15] People of colour have always been some of the most marginalised members of the working-class, at the sharpest end of societal and economic shocks. The 'white working class' narrative, then, serves no purpose other than to obscure where power lies, undermine liberatory politics, and reinstate the white male breadwinner as the default trade unionist and gatekeeper of the union.

---

13   Andy Beckett, When the Lights Went Out: Britain in the Seventies (London: Faber and Faber, 2010) p. 367.

14   https://jrf.org.uk/sites/default/files/jrf/migrated/files/2057.pdf (last accessed November 2020).

15   Beckett, *When the Lights Went Out*, p. 368.

Dawn Butler, member of Parliament for Brent Central and the third Black woman to become an MP when she was first elected in 2005, served as a full-time officer for the GMB union prior to her election, one of a minority of Black women officers. Reflecting on her time in the movement, Butler makes a distinction between a union's members and the model upon which it is built. 'Like most large organisations, trade union structures are very white and male dominated while the members are much more diverse,' she says. 'When I was working in the movement, it always felt like the movement wanted to embrace change. [But it] needs to diversify its processes and procedures.' Butler knows first-hand how conditional the solidarity of a trade union built in the breadwinner model can be: 'My most disappointing time as a member of the GMB was when the General Secretary refused to endorse me during my Labour Deputy Leadership campaign,' she tells me. 'I had worked for them for over ten years and contributed so much.'

The enduring appeal of the breadwinner model for certain sections of the movement is clear. Anyone from a minoritised or marginalised group who has been involved in left-wing activism and organising will likely be familiar with the many ways in which equality efforts are at times undermined in its defence. To highlight how women are uniquely and disproportionately affected by austerity is to divide the working class. Racism within the labour movement is a distraction that can be dealt with after the revolution. Advocating for disabled or LGBTQ+ representation in union structures is 'playing identity politics'. Migrants are competitors not comrades, taking jobs from the white working class, undercutting wages and driving down employment standards. These political fictions benefit only bosses. Our identities as women, as people of colour, as disabled people, migrants or members of the LGBTQ+ community are shaped by and shape how we experience our work and our class. They are foundations on which we can build and reinforce solidarity, not distractions through which it is eroded.

The limits of representation

Our white, male breadwinner has never been truly representative of Britain's working class, but his ascendancy coincided with the heyday of the labour movement in the UK, with the result that images of picket lines and marches dominated by white male labourers are often invoked as a platonic ideal for a movement working to rejuvenate itself. This nostalgia has a place; our predecessors deserve recognition for their victories and the movement that they built, and we can and should learn much from how they did it, while not ignoring the vital but often hidden role of marginalised workers throughout the labour movement's history. Many also remain involved today, willing to take radical solidarity actions with little to lose having long retired and paid off mortgages. But the breadwinner image remains as unrepresentative as ever. The most recent data available shows that women make up just under half of the UK workforce and just over half of all trade union members. People of colour account for 11.7 per cent of all workers and 9 per cent of all members. And disabled workers are more likely to be union members than their non-disabled counterparts, with 16.4 per cent of union members identifying as disabled compared to 14 per cent of all employees.[16]

In response to the ongoing hegemony of the breadwinner model and the clear injustice it has often given rise to, the UK's labour movement has made attempts to embrace equality and

16   https://tuc.org.uk/research-analysis/reports/tuc-equality-audit-2018?page=2 (last accessed November 2020).

diversity. Trade unions and the TUC include in their structures specific spaces and roles for marginalised workers: Black Workers' Committees, Women's Officers and Disabled Workers' networks, for example. These structures are designed to ensure representation, with spaces reserved on national committees for delegates from these groups. And they matter, because marginalised workers face both specific issues in the workplace – racism, homophobia, ableism, sexual harassment – as well as being disproportionately affected by general work issues such as low pay, insecurity and poor conditions. Campaigns on issues as wide-ranging as maternity leave, the BME pay gap, prayer space and non-binary recognition have been led and won by these networks and representatives, at all levels of the trade union movement. But too often they are still forced to operate in silos, the breadwinner model supposedly graciously accommodating them on the sidelines, but not stepping aside to let them into the fray.

This is because many unions built in the traditional model have internalised and reflected a societal understanding of equality that fails to reckon properly with power. At a societal level this can manifest as the misnomer that we should simply treat everybody the same, or that we 'shouldn't see' race or disability, for example. At a union level it can manifest as a belief, both subconscious and voiced, that race, gender, disability and sexuality cannot act as key organising principles of our lives, that they are add-ons, and that we do not need to reckon with the reality that social oppressions can have a formative role in shaping our class and working conditions. Equality and diversity initiatives, therefore, allow unions to respond to an increasingly diverse membership and some will to do 'the right thing', without compelling them to examine their own model or the distribution of power within it.

That the politics of equality and diversity, as opposed to liberation and justice, have also been increasingly corporatised and embraced by our bosses speaks to their limitations. While corporate equality efforts are undoubtedly driven by increasing societal pressure for organisations of all stripes to take these issues seriously, they also represent an inability to do so. As is evident in employment and economic inequalities, capitalism relies on and reinforces marginalisation and so our bosses, as actors of capitalism, do so too. Equality and diversity initiatives that prioritise representation over power, and optics over justice, then, provide corporations with an easy way to maximise profits through good PR while the power structures that maintain them remain intact.

But while corporations are actively invested in maintaining the status quo and have no role in redistributing power, the potential of unions to fight for a radically reorganised society is limitless. As we have explored, there are those within unions who also benefit from the power concentrated with, and often fiercely protected by, the white male breadwinner. But there are also many more with a genuine will to improve the lot of marginalised workers, including those workers themselves who have organised against the odds and made a material difference to their own lives and those of their peers. To truly mount a meaningful challenge against capital will be to put this work at the heart of union work, building a labour movement in a new model rather than accommodating diversity within the parameters of a broken one.

This mission will require unions to think differently about some of the most fundamental elements of their work and operations, and to back up the hard work being done on the ground by marginalised workers with a hard look at the structures within which they organise. To reach the most marginalised will be to devote resources to deep organising in unrecognised workplaces, acting to engage new members rather than simply responding to those who are long-standing. To truly listen and respond to what these workers have to say will be to reimagine union democratic structures and leadership in ways we will explore in more detail in Chapter 8. And to take seriously the ways in which our social oppressions interact with our class and our work will be to leverage traditional union tactics, and embrace new ones, behind issues which have previously been seen as fringe concerns. But the result will be a labour movement built on the strength of a working class united in its diversity and ready to take on capitalism in all its guises and at its roots.

Jo Grady, general secretary of the University and College Union and one of a minority of female trade union leaders in the UK, clearly highlights these limits of the labour movement's current approach, and the impetus for a liberatory unionism, when she tells me:

We're in a movement that's supposed to be at the forefront of fighting for and protecting people, but there's still a hierarchy of what's important. It's not acceptable for the union movement not to have a really reflective look at itself and ask whose interests it really fights for the hardest. In some sectors that will be securely employed people over casualised people, in some sectors that will be always talking about the gender pay gap but never talking about a BME pay gap, and in some sectors that will be weaponising feminism as a way to undermine the rights of trans women.

'I think if I could click my fingers,' she continues, 'it would be to bring everybody up to speed on how divisive that approach to emancipatory politics has been and will continue to be, and how it ends up feeding some of the very types of issues that we as a movement are trying to address.'

Towards liberatory unionism

In April 2019, when strip club dancers in Sheffield and Manchester found themselves the unwitting subjects of covert filming, it was their union they first turned to. Formed just a year earlier, the Sex Workers United (SWU) branch of United Voices of the World sprang into action to call out the violation and to seek legal recourse. The perpetrators? The Women's Equality Party, in a staggeringly misguided attempt to campaign against the existence of strip clubs.

That many elements of sex work remain criminalised legitimises a conditional solidarity from both the feminist movement and the workers' one, who can gift and withdraw their support based on their own moralising about womanhood and work. Despite the immediate dangers faced by a workforce dominated by society's most marginalised women, the majority of sex workers are unable to meaningfully unionise because their work is not yet recognised as such and they have no workers' rights to realise. Sex worker collectives like SWARM and the English Collective of Prostitutes have long campaigned for decriminalisation on this basis, arguing that moral assessments of sex work are irrelevant in a discussion about safety and rights. In their book *Revolting Prostitutes*, sex workers Molly Smith and Juno Mac write: 'A key struggle that sex workers face in feminist spaces is trying to move people past their sense of what prostitution *symbolises*, to grapple with what the criminalisation of prostitution *materially does* to people who sell sex . . . Nobody can build a better, more feminist world by treating sex workers' current material needs – for income, for safety from eviction, for safety from immigration enforcement – as trivial.'[17]

Yet still, certain sections of the feminist and workers' movements have consistently opposed the decriminalisation of sex work and the categorisation of it as work at all, holding sex workers to higher standards than almost any other workers over whether their work is empowering, aspirational or enjoyable. By contrast, an organising priority for the SWU branch of the United Voices of the World union is to achieve 'worker' status for the UK's sex workers, a classification which would make them eligible for employment rights and protections. The UVW were able to organise in this way, and respond quickly and effectively when its members were violated, because it has embraced unionism in a new model – entering unorganised workplaces, backing grassroots actions, and building structures in which members truly have power. The SWU also organises in partnership with sex worker support group x:talk and decriminalisation campaign Decrim Now, and therefore situate themselves at the intersection of feminist and workplace organising, making the case that it is more often than not austerity and poverty which cause women to enter sex work and therefore those forces which sex worker exclusionary feminists should instead rally against. Shortly after their establishment, the branch successfully opposed a discriminatory Deliveroo policy which banned the delivery of drinks to sex workers, characterising the clause as 'an attempt to pit precarious workers against one another'.[18] Sex workers urgently need the backing of a union movement

17   Molly Smith and Juno Mac, *Revolting Prostitutes* (London & New York: Verso, 2018) p. 108.
18   https://uvwunion.org.uk/en/news/2018/09/press-release-deliveroo-drops-discriminatory-policy-against-sex-workers-after-pressure-from-unions/ (last accessed April 2021).

recognising their work as work, echoing their calls for decriminalisation, and securing their basic rights, but there is no comfortable space for them in a unionism built in the breadwinner model. A liberatory unionism, by comparison, recognises as work this labour done primarily by marginalised women, and prioritises, in the words of Smith and Mac, the material circumstances they experience rather than a debate about what they symbolise.

Inspiration for a liberatory unionism can also be drawn from the USA, where healthcare access and benefits are often contingent on union membership and recognition. In her book *Out in the Union*, academic Miriam Frank makes one of the first attempts to document the efforts of queer organisers in advancing queer rights through collective bargaining: first, in the inclusion of sexual orientation in anti-discrimination clauses and then through the fight for equal domestic partner benefits in the 1990s and the ongoing battle for trans-inclusive healthcare and benefits to be included as part of contract negotiation.[19] Queer organisers in the USA have no choice but to engage with the ways in which their gender and sexual orientation shape their experience of work, because their health depends on it too.

And to think even bigger, a liberatory unionism must also be a global one that reckons with the role of borders and migration in reproducing class across the world. For unions in the UK, this means not only centring migrant workers in our organising, and forging international solidarity, but it also means considering our own role in systems of global exploitation, and standing together to oppose the UK's cruel and unjust immigration system and state violence enacted by the Home Office. A radical reorganisation of the labour movement in the interests of the

---

19   Miriam Frank, *Out in the Union: A Labor History of Queer America* (Philadelphia: Temple University Press, 2014).

most marginalised demands that British trade unionists develop a critique of imperialism, vehemently rejecting any notion of migrants as threatening or subordinate and instead organising alongside them as part of a united international working class.

In detention centres, for example, as described by Franck Magennis and Isaac Ricca-Richardson of the Legal Sector Workers United branch of United Voices of the World,[20] detainees regularly undertake low-paid and exploitative work[21] under the guise of 'paid activity', spun by the Home Office as an opportunity for recreation and intellectual stimulation.[22] A liberatory labour movement of the type envisaged by Magennis and Ricca-Richardson could see unions take their place alongside migrant and refugee rights groups to call for the complete closure of these inhumane facilities in the long-term, while also recognising this activity as work and organising detainees themselves as workers to improve conditions in the present.

A liberatory unionism, then, is one in which sex workers are organised and have a seat at the table to discuss their working conditions and not their morality. It is a unionism in which the specific needs of women, disabled, queer and Black workers can be advanced through collective bargaining. Just imagine the potential if unions leveraged their strength behind progressive immigration reform, if unpaid carers were organised, or if medical leave for trans workers transitioning was seen as an industrial action issue for a whole branch. If unions are prepared to work in the interests of the most marginalised and not just the

---

20 https://novaramedia.com/2020/05/25/detained-migrants-are-workers-they-belong-in-the-trade-union-movement/ (last accessed May 2021).

21 https://independent.co.uk/news/uk/home-news/coronavirus-travel-ban-uk-detention-deportation-home-office-legal-challenge-a9522811.html (last accessed May 2021).

22 https://legislation.gov.uk/uksi/2001/238/article/17/made (last accessed May 2021).

best represented, entering unorganised workplaces and over-hauling democratic structures, they can be a liberatory force. Today's young workers are part of the most diverse working class this country has ever seen, and arguably care more strongly than any generation before them about human rights and liber-ation.[23] Across the country, young people are engaging in work that acknowledges and responds to the intersection between our class and other oppressions, whether through mutual aid groups, feminist organising, radical queer spaces or elsewhere. The role for the labour movement now must be to embrace a radical reor-ganising in which this work can be union work, backed up by all the legal protection, organising experience, political education and institutional knowledge that brings.

---

23 https://therenewalproject.com/these-are-the-causes-gen-z-cares-about-the-most/ (last accessed November 2020).

Chapter 5

HR are not your friends

I once worked for a third sector organisation where the director, who was active on national Fair Work task forces, said that he would feel he had failed as a boss if his workforce wanted to unionise. His majority-female workers, shunted constantly between different short-term contracts and in the face of low pay and endless restructures, did want to unionise, but to this day have not yet managed it. There was a staff committee, we were told. Raise it with the employee voice representative, we were told. You should feel like the management is approachable and amenable, we were told. These are just some of a litany of protestations unions and their members regularly face when trying to gain official recognition or raise a grievance. They may appear less hostile than overt union-busting activities or a slammed door in the face, but they can amount to something more insidious altogether – something I have come to term 'corporate creep'. Capital has always dictated the terms within which we discuss labour, but as the power of unions has waned and neoliberalism has accelerated, its actors have developed ever-more duplicitous and cynical means by which to do so. Corporate creep describes this; the process by which the spheres of workers' rights are co-opted or undermined by employers, corporations and private individuals, almost always with vested interests in disempowering them. It can take many forms, as we'll go on to see, but its ultimate outcome is always to make unions seem unnecessary, obscuring their unique position as independent and protected entities and thereby removing some of their power.

One of the most widespread and overt ways in which this occurs might be in the positioning of Human Resources (HR) departments. Anyone who has ever worked in a reasonably sized company will be familiar with the induction drill: here's your locker; that's your manager; if you have any problems just contact HR. Workers are consistently sold the idea that HR are their champions and guardians in the workplace, there to mediate conflict, ensure well-being and generally look after their staff. In actual fact, you only have to take a second glance at the name to understand that this is artifice. Far from the soft, people-focussed role HR has come to occupy in the public imagination, its purpose is to utilise the role of humans – workers – as resources in pursuit of an organisation's wider strategic objectives. Insofar as keeping your staff happy makes sense for maintaining a productive and docile workforce, HR are our champions. But shorter hours, higher pay, more control? That's not in the purview of a department with our employer's interests at heart.

Melanie Simms, Professor of Work and Employment at the University of Glasgow, says this (mis)understanding of the role of HR is so pervasive as to occasionally surprise even those who begin training in it, believing it to be more akin to counselling or customer service than strategic planning and operations:

'An HR discussion which was about "how can we make sure our employees aren't annoyed by this strategic decision we're making?" would be regarded as being an employee champion, rather than saying "we think all this profit should be redistributed in the form of pay," for example,' she explains. 'Even the most "employee champion" oriented HR manager is not looking to overthrow capitalism, but to help the organisation get to where they want to go.'

This distinction gets to the heart of what is a common retort to unions and organising: the idea that there are bad bosses, yes, but there are good ones too. And while it's true that there are nice people in management positions, with their own bills to pay and families to feed, it's also undeniably true that they have more power than, and different objectives from, the workers underneath them. They also have orders to carry out from the bosses above them. People move around and through workplaces: managers leave, co-workers get promoted, teams get restructured. Faces change, but the power dynamic remains intact.

Who gets in the room?

There's one reason why bosses love teamwork but hate unions: they know that collective action works. The former takes place on their terms while the latter fundamentally challenges those terms. Teamwork in the workplace gets an organisation closer to its aims while unionisation might be in direct conflict with them. Capitalism demands of us that we live, work and act as increasingly atomised individuals, solitarily navigating an ever more complex society and labour market in which our bosses have ultimate control. Team building does not by definition undermine that control, but unionising does.

Initiatives such as Employee Voice Committees similarly take place on an employer's terms. Ostensibly a space where workers can advance their interests, they are generally initiated and have their frameworks dictated by managers or HR departments, with no promise of confidentiality or discretion. They also have little power, with bosses under no obligation to do more than pay lip service to the suggestions coming out of such meetings. On executive boards, where power is concentrated, workers have little voice. The labour movement has long lobbied for reserved spaces for workers on boards, a move which would be very welcome – but which still offers little challenge to the fundamental power imbalance. Without a strong union, a worker on a board is vulnerable to being railroaded against their interests, with an employer able to point to their inclusion as a way of legitimising decisions of all kinds. And why, a particularly cynical boss might say, should the organisation recognise a union when David from Accounts has a seat on the board?

Likewise, workers often get a place at the table through membership of professional associations – the Chartered Institute of Public Relations or the Institute of Directors, for example – rather than unions. These quasi-unions similarly stake a claim to advancing the collective voice of a workforce but similarly do so on the employer's terms. Much like HR, these associations often seek to promote the reputation of a profession or to ensure harmony between workers and bosses to the benefit of a brand. Many take laudable positions on workplace issues and work productively alongside unions where these interests intersect, but they should not be understood as a viable alternative. Like HR and employee voice committees, these associations get in the room by being actors of capitalism instead of opponents to it.

In response to cross-sector issues, workers can also sometimes try to forge a voice for themselves through the establishment of single-issue campaigns. These can be necessary and are often effective, emerging by means similar to the process of union organising. However workers choose to collectivise their grievances and form a workers' voice should be welcomed, but to choose this route is to miss out on the benefits of a union: legal protection; institutional knowledge; a united front. In relation to my own industry of freelance journalism, for example, a plethora of campaigns with similar-sounding names and overlapping objectives sprung up in response to a lack of support for self-employed people during the Coronavirus pandemic. While extremely worthwhile, this cluttered landscape made it difficult for individual workers to know who to get behind, with many likely foregoing involvement out of confusion. More insidiously, a collection of similar groups without an overarching alliance creates a good excuse for decision-makers not to listen to any. The best home for campaigns of this nature, therefore, remains a trade union.

The growth of the career economy

The timeline of the 2010s and the proliferation of digital and social media has corporate creep shot through its middle like a stick of rock. In 2013, Facebook Chief Operating Officer Sheryl Sandberg published *Lean In*, a sort of manual for working women about how they might entirely change themselves to succeed in leadership at work. The following year, Sophia Amoruso, founder of the Nasty Gal online clothing brand, released *#GIRLBOSS*, described by Lena Dunham as 'more than a book . . . a movement'.[1] Fast forward a couple of years to 2017 and bombshell allegations of sexual harassment against Harvey Weinstein: the subsequent #MeToo hashtag launched a thousand hot takes, with Twitter threads, personal essays and Instagram infographics addressing how women could best realise their rights in the workplace – almost never through unions and collective action, and almost always through yogic breathing, HR reps and individualised complaints procedures in a seemingly fictional world

---

1   https://waterstones.com/book/girlboss/sophia-amoruso/9780241217931 (last accessed April 2021).

where a worker can simply book a private meeting with their boss in which to state their case.

In 2018, writer Emma Gannon's *Multi-Hyphen Method* highlighted how the digital age has enabled millennials to curate their own careers, while Natalie Alzate topped podcast charts with *#Viral*, in which the YouTuber and self-described entrepreneur interviews 'established and emerging digital stars . . . about their goals, approach, successes, failures and secrets to how they got where they are.'[2] A year later, Anne Helen Peterson's Buzzfeed essay 'How Millennials Became the Burnout Generation'[3] became a viral sensation just months before academic Melissa A. Fabello's controversial tweet about the 'emotional labour' of supporting friends was shared nearly 10,000 times and dissected in almost as many online essays.

That our dissatisfaction with work has become such a profitable business is both bitterly ironic while not wholly surprising. As a nation, our mental health has deteriorated rapidly since the 1990s[4] with 16 to 24-year-old women among the worst affected, and work repeatedly cited as a key source of stress. Issues of bullying, discrimination and harassment are gradually becoming less taboo, and women in particular have been encouraged through zeitgeist feminism to open up about their experiences instead of grinning and bearing them. It's little coincidence that the career economy is largely feminised and aggressively marketed at millennial women.

---

2   https://open.spotify.com/show/7Eo09SdEl6o8SkQdgxpmQl (last accessed April 2021).

3   https://buzzfeednews.com/article/annehelenpetersen/millennials-burnout-generation-debt-work (last accessed April 2021).

4   https://mind.org.uk/information-support/types-of-mental-health-problems/statistics-and-facts-about-mental-health/how-common-are-mental-health-problems/#AreMentalHealthProblemsIncreasing (last accessed November 2020).

But just as much of that zeitgeist feminism has neglected an analysis of power and structure in favour of encouraging individual women to find answers within themselves. The career economy offers little by way of interrogating the role of bosses or capital in our dissatisfaction, or offering collective solutions to it. Increasingly, business and work have opened up as avenues for the influencer industry, with social media personalities shilling online courses, workbooks and coaching to their audiences for thousands of pounds at a time, whether they are qualified to do so or not. In 2020, journalist Vicky Spratt wrote about so-called Instagram business coach Sarah Akwisombe and the women who had paid thousands of pounds to her 'No Bull Business School'.[5] 'I thought I was buying business advice but it wasn't anything I didn't already know,' said one client. 'The focus was mainly on mindset and . . . advice like getting up at five in the morning and doing loads of cardio, or getting rid of people in your life who don't support you.' No amount of business coaching, Instagram-aestheticised career books, or cardiovascular exercise can compete with a union. The problem is not our mindset, our access to productivity software or our propensity to hit the snooze button – it is the uneven distribution of power and wealth. Those challenges are collective, not individual, and for this reason only unions are equipped to answer them.

The career economy, and the corporate creep it is symbolic of, has been able to flourish in the space left by weakened unions and the erosion of collectivism. It is a phenomenon that can also be seen in the growing self-care industry: if you search for '#selfcare' on Instagram on any given day, you will be immediately bombarded by over 1 million results. You'll scroll through images of skinny white women in yoga inversions, of bubble baths

---

5   https://refinery29.com/en-gb/money-manifesting-life-coaching-instagram (last accessed November 2020).

and hot chocolate, of self-care journals, kits and workbooks you can click through to buy. You might, if you're lucky, scroll past an Audre Lorde quote, pasted in an aesthetically pleasing font against a pastel background: 'Caring for myself is not self-indulgence, it is self-preservation.' Lorde actually followed this statement with 'and that is an act of political warfare,' although that part is often left out, presumably so as not to upset the corporations cashing in on our collective insecurities. Despite its origins in activism and organising, the concept of self-care has now become squarely co-opted by capital through means akin to corporate creep, and it's little wonder why. The phrase's popularity has exploded in recent years as inequalities have widened, capitalism's grip has tightened, and global politics have looked extremely volatile. As people search for answers, capitalism sells them false consciousness: bath bombs and mason jars on the surface, individualism and atomisation underneath.

It is in capitalism's interests to deepen the gulf between care for ourselves as individuals, and the obligation we have to care for our communities. Defined by community organiser Nikita Valerio as 'people committed to leveraging their privilege to be there for one another in various ways,'[6] community care compels us to acknowledge how intricately our own actions and well-being are wrapped up with those of others, in direct opposition to the individualism of capitalist self-care. When the Coronavirus pandemic hit, for example, individual responsibility wasn't enough to keep us safe, and mutual aid sprung up as an alternative to an ailing welfare state. Capitalism's power relies on us being alone, competitive and doubting our own abilities, and its tools, the self-care industry included, operate to keep us that way. Joining a union builds the collective strength to take

6   https://mashable.com/article/community-care-versus-self-care/?europe=true (last accessed April 2021).

on capital, but it also helps us to resist its impacts: creating friendships and alliances centred on a politics of care; building confidence; insisting on fun and joy in the face of our struggles.

Workers' education

While the career economy sells us personal branding courses and goal-setting worksheets, meaningful workers' education is under threat. In October 2020, a week after Prime Minister Boris Johnson announced plans for a 'Lifetime Skills Guarantee' which would see eligible adult learners offered fully funded courses as part of the Coronavirus response, the TUC received a surprise email from Skills Minister Gillian Keegan: with no warning signs, the government was to completely scrap funding for the Union Learning Fund (ULF), effective immediately from the close of the financial year the following March.

The ULF, established in 1998 and worth around £11m a year, had previously supported 200,000 workers each year to access workplace learning and training, ranging from basic literacy, numeracy and ICT skills to apprenticeships, traineeships and continuous professional development. In 2018, an evaluation[7] found that 68 per cent of learners with no previous qualifications earned one, and 80 per cent gained skills they could take with them to future other jobs.[8] For every £1 spent on the Learning Fund, employers gained £4.70 in increased productivity, and the net contribution of the ULF to the economy was estimated at more than £1.4 billion. Its impacts were clear: the scheme more than paid for itself, it improved people's lives, it

---

7   https://tuc.org.uk/news/employers-and-unions-unite-call-protect-brilliant-and-vital-union-learning-fund (last accessed November 2020).

8   https://tuc.org.uk/news/employers-and-unions-unite-call-protect-brilliant-and-vital-union-learning-fund (last accessed November 2020).

received good feedback. Why would a government committed to 'building back better' and 'levelling up' want to scrap it?

The answer may lie more with ideology than with efficiency. Nobody could doubt the cost-effectiveness or success of the scheme, but it was brokered by unions and served to empower working people. Despite its obvious contributions, it fell victim to a suspicion and hostility towards unions as institutions of solidarity which threaten profits and bosses, and stand in the way of the society Conservatives would seek to create. So strong was that hostility that depriving workers of the skills they need to survive was just necessary collateral damage.

Working class access to education has always been conditional and contested along these lines. The labour movement, by way of response, has a long history of supporting lifelong learning, opening up a world of possibilities to those locked out of traditional education by their means, qualifications, self-doubt or horizons. Traditional rhetoric would have us believe that education is a means of escaping the working class, but workers' education allows us to learn on our own terms, using the skills we gain to strengthen our class rather than seeking to somehow 'rise' out of it. That vision is radical, but it is also vital for the advancement of the working class. As the movement contends with the changing world of work, for example, accessible learning opportunities will be essential. If automation is to change the nature of our jobs, we must be able to retrain and gain transferable skills, at no cost and in work time. As unions have tried to face up to their decline with service and partnership models, mission creep has permeated the concept of lifelong learning. Often it is sold to workers as career development, and to governments and employers as a drive to affordably upskill the workforce. It is both of these things. But we must also remember and defend its radical roots: education as a liberatory force that working-class people deserve as much as their privileged peers, and one which can bolster our movement.

For the love of the job?

VICE Media has always been synonymous with youth, grit and edginess. But when workers in the US arm of the business began speaking out in 2017, they told a tale as old as time: a sleazy culture of sexual misconduct permeated, enabled in part by a requirement for all new employees to sign a 'non-traditional workplace agreement' which stipulated that 'although it is possible that some of the text, images and information I will be exposed to in the course of my employment with VICE may be considered by some to be offensive, indecent, violent or disturbing, I do not find such text, images or information or the workplace environment at VICE to be offensive, indecent, violent or disturbing.'[9,10]

The specific inclusion of 'the workplace environment' in the contract shrouded bosses in impunity, said staff, who described male managers openly referencing the clause before making sexually inappropriate comments. Those implicated have since been removed from their positions, the non-traditional workplace agreement scrapped, and a union recognised voluntarily by the company – but that it ever existed can still teach us a lot about the strategies used by bosses to revel in their own power while reducing that of their workers to respond.

9   https://thedailybeast.com/unsafe-and-just-plain-dirty-women-accuse-vice-of-toxic-sexual-harassment-culture (last accessed November 2020).

10   It should be noted that I have worked for VICE UK on a freelance basis on numerous occasions since 2017, on the understanding that these allegations were dealt with comprehensively at the time and that the non-traditional workplace clause no longer exists. In 2019, workers at VICE UK unionised and were recognised voluntarily by their employer.

The notion that certain workplaces are uniquely fun, quirky, informal or honourable can operate to obscure poor practices and pave the way for union-busting by stealth.

Workplaces like VICE are renowned for their perks and informal office culture, with rumours rife about pick'n'mix bars, skateboards in the office, Friday desk beers and a 'work hard, play harder' ethos that pervades the business. As technology and insecurity have worked to blur boundaries between work and leisure to the benefit of bosses, many have embraced these so-called perks in what looks like an attempt to be a 'good' employer but which ultimately amounts to a further shoring up of power and the encroaching of work on the rest of a worker's life. Free breakfasts might seem generous, but don't they make you feel like you should eat at your desk? Is boardroom yoga at lunchtime a perk, or does it amount to another hour of would-be leisure time spent in the office? An unlimited holiday allowance might present the illusion of freedom and trust, but if your colleague is praised for foregoing his leave, will you feel able to take yours?

This can be a difficult line for trade unionists to draw: isn't our role, after all, to advocate for workers? Shouldn't we welcome benefits and perks? Don't we want our days to be more bearable? But trade unionists should deal in the material circumstances that improve our conditions and our lives, and not in gimmicks and distractions. In many cases, these ploys act as a smokescreen for a patchwork of poor and undercooked policies around issues like sick leave, mental health and equality, or as a retort to 'ungrateful' workers who dare to raise grievances. It's no surprise, for example, that 'mindfulness' seemed to enter the HR lexicon around the same time as employers responded to austerity by freezing or worsening their pay, terms and conditions. By all means we can enjoy the ping-pong table at the staff fun day, but we might want to consider first what it might be obscuring.

Some employers have gone so far down this route as to brand themselves as a 'home from home' or a 'second family'. But most of us already have a home and a family, both of which we are likely at work to pay for, and both of which we would appreciate spending more undivided time with. Austin Kelmore had been working in the video games industry for twelve years when he was unceremoniously sacked by developer Ustwo in 2019, in what IWGB Game Workers, a branch of the IWGB, say was a clear case of unfair dismissal when the self-described 'fampany' (a portmanteau of 'family' and 'company') accused him of spending too much time championing diversity and challenging bosses. 'It feels that Austin is a self-appointed bastion of change and sometimes speaks on behalf of others,' read an email obtained by the *Guardian*.[11] 'The studio runs as a collective "we" rather than leadership v employees, which may have been Austin's experience in the past, but it's not how things are here.'

Jaime Cross, IWGB Game Workers' branch secretary, tells me that the construction of video games as a 'passion industry' – that is, one in which workers consider themselves to be paid for a hobby or cause they already care about or enjoy – has laid the groundwork for much of this hostility towards unions. Robust contracts are few and far between and start-up culture is widespread, with new businesses regularly popping up with little infrastructure or experience behind them. 'There's very much a "we're all in this together" mentality at both large and small companies,' he explains.

---

11   https://theguardian.com/politics/2019/oct/03/ustwo-austin-kelmore-union-organiser-sacked-games (last accessed November 2020).

If you're doing overtime, everybody's doing overtime. That mentality pervades to other more established companies: you've got to be there and take it for the team. People's social dynamics are kind of based on 'why did you leave at the end of the day?' And people will negatively perceive others for making that choice of wanting to have their own life.

Video game development might seem to have little in common with the violence against women sector, but similar sentiments were also expressed to me by workers attempting to unionise the latter with United Voices of the World. When they launched the first ever UK union branch for gender-based violence workers in 2019, one organiser told me that the obvious care she and colleagues had for their work and clients had been leveraged against them by bosses trying to crack down on union activities. Corporate creep exists in all sectors and in many shapes and sizes, including the cynical deployment of perks and quirks in place of rights and protections, and in the manipulation of workers by way of their own interests and compassion. As Jaime Cross puts it, 'everybody's a family until somebody needs something or you're a nuisance'.

Corporate creep is so ubiquitous as to seem initially unremarkable. In early research for this book I found myself googling search terms like 'worker boss relationship' or 'rights at work', seeking out results from trade union websites or academic essays, and instead being met with listicles outlining 'Top Ten Management Techniques From HR Professionals' or personal essays in women's magazines about 'ditching the nine-to-five and building a career that works for you!' Everywhere we look, bosses create the illusion of giving voice and power to their workers, while opposing the unions which would give them actual power, on their own terms. The co-option of public conversation about work and workers' rights by private corporations and individuals has been impressively effective, with the labour movement not even invited to the discussion at times. And the allure of corporate creep is strong: HR is built into the fabric of our workplaces and social media promises us self-improvement at the click of a button and without leaving home. But these only seem like the easiest options for confronting our dissatisfaction because capitalism wants us to believe that they are. The labour movement's task is to reach those who would naturally turn to an employee voice committee or a self-styled career coach and meet them with political education and deep organising. Despite these attempts to undermine their power, unions remain the only viable way to take on capital and our bosses know it.

Chapter 6

Transcending the workplace

Look through a union archive, and sooner or later you'll find a poster emblazoned with a slogan about how the unions invented the weekend or fought for the eight-hour day. These wins were real, hard-won, and they established a baseline for how workers should be treated across the country – of course we should be proud of them. But they also emerged in a labour market and a society profoundly different from the one we find ourselves in today. Does the establishment of the weekend, won in the 1930s, resonate with a hospitality worker for whom Fridays and Saturdays are the busiest shifts of the week? Does the nine-teenth century slogan of 'eight hours for work, eight hours for rest, eight hours for recreation' mean anything to precarious and zero-hour workers waiting for the phone to ring – or the app to buzz – at any given moment? Does a slogan so focussed on work even feel relevant to a young person, whose most pressing concerns engulf them at home too?

Today's young workers find themselves in a world where the lines between work, rest and recreation are increasingly blurred and where the challenges facing them are existential in nature and go far beyond the workplace. A public health crisis which threatens the fabric of society; a climate crisis which threatens the future of the planet; a housing crisis which threatens our immediate and long-term prosperity. None of these crises can be separated from each other and nor can they be separated from the realm of work or the issues facing us as we undertake it. The future of union organising, then, is not just within, but also beyond the workplace. To achieve their full potential as vehicles for a radical redistribution of power, unions must be prepared to embrace 'social movement unionism', forging alliances with other collectives, campaigning on wider societal issues, and situating themselves within a wider movement for social justice in all its forms.

Unions in the community

'We're about building power; we always want to build it bigger and bigger,' says Anny Cullum, national organiser at ACORN (The Association of Community Organisations for Reform Now) community union.

We feel like you can boil down the ordinary person's problems to a lack of power in society. There's power that comes from having loads of money and wealth, and there's power that comes from having the numbers. We want to organise people into a strong union where they can upskill, be accountable to each other and build power to address our problems.

ACORN, established in Bristol in 2014, is a national union which exists to organise communities rather than workplaces, fighting for a better quality of life for all citizens. In the years since its inception the union has grown into a national body, modelling its structures on those of trade unions with members and branches across the country, and winning on issues ranging from evictions and social housing to Universal Credit, green energy and childcare provision. The growth of ACORN and its continued commitment from young members has happened in spite of the weakening power of trade unions and their struggle to attract younger workers. Its comparative strength speaks to the enduring appeal of collectivism and the politicisation of young people, while suggesting that a union with its roots in wider society might be more relatable to young workers than one wedded solely to the workplace.

In 2017, ACORN Bristol members spotted a consultation on scrapping council tax exemption for people on low incomes, a move that would have affected 25,000 of the poorest households in the city. Immediately they shot into action, an agile organising model allowing them to bypass bureaucracy and head straight for the doorstep, with members partaking in door-knocking sessions, mass consultation responses and direct actions at local councillors' surgeries. Built into the ACORN model is a balance between proactivity – going out into the community to learn about shared concerns – and being able to respond reactively to issues as they emerge. Grievances are collectivised and seen as an opportunity for political education; rather than continually defending single members, others affected within the community are identified and their issues are woven into wider narratives about injustice and power. And members retain ownership over campaigns, being encouraged to pitch in with organising strategy and on-the-ground work rather than relying on a representative to do it on their behalf, as might be expected in a more traditional union. In Bristol in 2017, this model proved itself: the city's mayor dropped his planned cuts, Bristol became the only major city to retain the full reduction, and £4m of public money stayed in the pockets of those who needed it most.

Trade unions across the country have lent their support to ACORN, donating funds and formalising affiliations between local branches. ACORN members speak at trade union events about their organising strategies and vice versa, and both sides encourage members to join and get involved with the other. For Anny Cullum, this is the future of the union movement. 'I think we have to cooperate and defer to each other's specialities,' she says. 'There's a gap in trade union models that can work on issues in the community, but ACORN can fill it. We need to work together and encourage each other's growth.' A community unionism built on partnership between the labour movement and collectives such as ACORN matters because workers exist beyond their workplaces, and working-class solidarity can be built on fronts other than labour. It is effective because all the principles of trade unionism can be applied in other contexts and against other manifestations of capital. And it is essential, because each of those manifestations reinforces the others. Workers are citizens, tenants and community members; a mass working-class movement should mobilise them in all the forms in which they exist.

Organising renters

At Govan Cross, in south-west Glasgow, stands a statue of Mary Barbour. A community activist and key figure in the Red Clydeside movement of the early twentieth century, Barbour is best known for leading Govan's women in a successful 1915 rent strike after landlords tried to capitalise on an influx of wartime shipbuilders and munitions factory workers by raising rents. They imagined that the women, left home while their husbands fought in the war, would be polite and amenable, but they weren't banking on Barbour's community organising skills or fearless determination.

More than 100 years later, at 9 a.m. on 24 August 2019, Barbour's statue looked on as activists and organisers gathered around her to begin a 'day of action'. Some were refuse collection workers from the GMB, one of the UK's oldest and largest trade unions, and some were members of Living Rent, a tenants' union established by university students in 2014. All were there to take direct action against budget cuts by Glasgow City Council, which had left refuse collection workers underpaid and overworked, and backyards across Govan filthy, strewn with rubbish, and infested by rodents. Activists dispersed to clean up yards across the neighbourhood, promising to meet back at noon with the rubbish they had collected, for a demonstration against the cuts.[1]

'That was a great moment,' says Emma Saunders, national organiser at Living Rent, of the Govan action. 'I think that's where I see the future: finding common issues around public services, transport, better housing and so on that we can team up on. I think members in both organisations benefit and learn from it, and that's the only way we'll build the power we need to.'

Living Rent began as a tenants' rights campaign, but restructured in 2016 to become a union when members began to feel they had reached the limits of what a campaign model could accomplish. 'We weren't going to have enough power to achieve the demands we needed, and it was always going to be the same group of 20–30 activists, often politicised people with social and cultural capital,' explains Saunders. 'It was about how we could

---

1   In December 2020, after a prolonged campaign by Living Rent and the GMB, Glasgow City Council agreed to talks over refuse collection issues in the area. At the time of writing, no agreement has been reached.

get more people to have ownership over victories, and the sense of empowerment that comes from changing things.'

This ethos underpins other grassroots tenants movements across the UK, including the London Renters' Union who part-nered in 2020 with the British Medical Association, and others including ACORN and Living Rent, to warn of the increased risk of COVID-19 for homeless people and those in poor housing. Tenant and trade unions have worked effectively together across the country where they have been able to organise on the basis of shared interests and shared opponents, beginning from a place of material circumstance rather than bureaucratic faction-alism. 'I'm interested in just starting with reality and the issues, and fighting for specific things,' says Saunders. 'When you get hung up on idealism and vision and doing things the perfect way it doesn't give you the small victories and feedback you need to sustain your energy.'

Climate justice as a trade union issue

Issue-based unions operating outside of the workplace have huge contributions to make to the union movement and the building of working-class power, but traditional trade unions have a role in wider social movements too. For a start, most issues are labour issues: underpaid and overworked carers lead to poorer care standards; overburdened teachers can't give students the best education they deserve; tired and exploited train drivers are more likely to cause accidents. Established trade unions have experience, resources and strength that they should be ready to leverage behind these kinds of social causes.

Simon Hannah, Joint Branch Secretary for Lambeth Unison, was among those who took notice immediately when a burgeon-ing climate justice movement started making waves in the shape of school strikes and direct action by Extinction Rebellion. While many members of the latter reject any relationship between capitalism and climate change, for Hannah the link has long been clear. 'I think capitalism is the main driver of climate change – a carbon economy where profit is the primary motive,' he tells me. 'So that means workers have got a really powerful position within the capitalist mode of production to stop the system, overflow the system, take control of the system and change it. It's only when we activate working people in their position as workers and not just as citizens that we can really begin to tackle the problem.'

Hannah's branch set about forming alliances with the climate justice movement, passing motions at branch level in support of school strikes and inviting Extinction Rebellion activists to speak to their members. In September 2019, the union secured paid time off for members to attend a protest organised by climate strikers, where they marched with a Lambeth Unison banner alongside school students and environmental activists. As well as the everyday work of advancing climate justice in the workplace, including persuading managers to sign up to a charter and pushing for a 4-day week to cut carbon emissions, the branch's visibility on an urgent social and global issue saw new members sign up and take on active roles within the union.

Not everyone in the labour movement has been quick to agree with Hannah. Its foundations in heavy industry and manual labour have meant a high density of union members in industries still reliant on fossil and dirty fuels, and the reactionary, self-protectionist culture cultivated by attacks on unions has seen some jump to protect polluting jobs over working to halt runaway climate change. Some workers in the transport and aviation sectors, for example, have been reticent to get behind what they see as a threat to their livelihoods. In response, more environmentally conscious parts of the labour movement have responded with the slogan 'there are no jobs on a dead planet'.

But among the progressive labour movement is a growing understanding that the only conscionable response is a 'Green New Deal' or 'green industrial revolution', with workers supported to reskill smoothly into low-carbon, well-paid and unionised jobs in a 'just transition'. The Labour Party's 2019 manifesto, for example, pledged a sevenfold increase in publicly owned offshore wind by 2030 and the return of profits to under-invested coastal areas in a plan that would have created 70,000 low-carbon, high-skilled and unionised jobs within a decade.[2] The aims of trade unionism and those of climate justice are mutually reinforcing rather than in conflict, and a future which improves the lot of both is not beyond us. For Lambeth Unison, voicing this perspective in chorus with climate strikers and environmental protestors has been an invaluable recruitment tool as well as a source of solidarity. The issue of climate justice shows us that only by thinking beyond our own workplaces can trade unionists reach the right conclusions and remain relevant to prospective members.

A global struggle

At first glance, the 2018 documentary *Nae Pasaran* appears to tell the story of a group of trade unionists in 1970s East Kilbride, Scotland. But its scope, it emerges, is much broader altogether: Around 7,000 miles away from the area's famous Rolls Royce factory, a military coup led by Chile's General Pinochet (and supported by Margaret Thatcher) is underway. When Chilean Air Force jet engines arrive at the factory, furious trade unionist

---

2   https://labour.org.uk/press/peoples-power-labour-announces-plan-offshore-windfarms-public-stake/ (last accessed February 2021).

Bob Fulton, backed by his co-workers, refuses to repair them and the parts sit rusting in a field behind the factory.

The workers never learned what impact their quiet solidarity had until the making of the documentary more than 40 years on, when they were presented with thank you messages from Chilean prisoners, exiles and torture victims who, unbeknownst to them, had heard of their action at the time. The engines they had grounded, it transpires, had been the very same to have bombed the presidential palace a year earlier in one of the conflict's bloodiest and most notorious showdowns.

As *Nae Pasaran*'s heroes themselves point out in the film, global solidarity of this nature would be almost impossible under today's restrictive anti-union laws and insecure employment contracts. But it demonstrates both the impetus for social movement unionism, and the fact that such unionism is always necessarily global in nature. General Pinochet's reign is long over, but authoritarianism is on the rise throughout the world. Globalisation means people working side-by-side with migrant workers, and within complex supply chains that weave around the planet. Black Lives Matter protests began in America and spread across the world as nations on different continents began to reckon with how their own societies are structured around anti-Blackness. We live global lives; our oppressions are global in nature, so our battles must be too.

International solidarity within the British labour movement can take many forms. It can mean sharing resources and expertise, as Thomson's Solicitors, the country's leading trade union lawyers, did in 2003 when they helped South African miners and their families win a £45 million settlement for asbestos exposure during apartheid, and then supported Johannesburg lawyers to set up their own trade union law firm. It can mean raising our collective voice in support of struggles elsewhere, as the TUC did in 2020 when it denounced attacks on Colombian trade unionists following a national strike the year previous. It could mean affiliating to the Boycott, Divestment and Sanctions movement in support of Palestinian liberation, or pushing your own employer for transparency in their supply chains and procurement processes. It will always mean acknowledging our role in meeting global exploitation with global working-class solidarity.

Bargaining for the common good

In the USA, a new model has emerged from the labour movement to align workers' struggles with community issues and the pursuit of social justice. 'Bargaining for the common good' is an alliance of unions, community and student groups, and racial justice organisations – from cleaners' unions to the local vegetable delivery cooperative – committed to working together to 'build long-term community-labor power, not [just] give unions some good publicity during a contract fight.'[3] Among key principles is the engagement of community allies in bargaining campaigns, and the centring of racial justice in demands.

The model was put to the test in 2019 when the Chicago Teachers Union (CTU) coordinated strike action with other school unions and campaign groups like Black Lives Matter, on the basis that 'education justice is racial justice,' a reference to how disproportionately poor educational access and outcomes for Black and brown children affect the rest of their lives. Almost 30,000 workers across the city walked out for eleven days, going far beyond traditional union demands to fight for multilingual education and expanded English language teaching.

3   https://bargainingforthecommongood.org/about/ (last accessed November 2020).

And they didn't stop there, calling for nurses, counsellors and social workers in schools and an increase in affordable housing for teachers, parents and students. Their broad-based alliance inspired huge public support from across the labour movement and beyond and proved too powerful for the city's authorities to resist: at the culmination of the strike, Mayor Lori Lightfoot committed to pay rises, reduced class sizes, and the hiring of more nurses and social workers.[4] The Chicago teachers operate under some of the most restrictive anti-union laws in America, with a 2011 Illinois law requiring the CTU to receive support from 75 per cent of all members (not just of those voting) in order to strike, and stipulations which mean the things they bargain on are not all technically subject to legal bargaining.[5] In the UK, we are similarly limited by the outlawing of political or solidarity strikes and by legal requirements for industrial action to concern narrow and specific issues, if indeed it is to make it past draconian balloting requirements in the first place. Chicago, therefore, shows us what can be possible even in the face of seemingly insurmountable barriers: building alliances and narratives, mobilising collectives and communities of all kinds in pursuit of justice.

Imagine for a moment a cleaners' campaign at a university; a predominantly female, Latin American migrant workforce, calling not only for better pay and conditions but also for an end to the Home Office's 'hostile environment'. Imagine these demands being backed by lecturers' and students' unions who understand the impact a cleaner's exploitation has on their work and education, and by racial and migrant justice groups

---

4 https://reuters.com/article/us-chicago-education-idUSKBN1XA12Y (last accessed April 2021).

5 https://labornotes.org/2012/10/how-chicago-teachers-got-organized-strike (last accessed June 2021).

who recognise the harms of the hostile environment on all those they fight for. Imagine feminist groups coming on board in an age-old fight for domestic work to be valued. Imagine a community union like ACORN mobilising local citizens: fellow migrants who share the same struggles, British neighbours invested in living with clean surroundings. Imagine a tenants' union like Living Rent making the case that hostile environment policies empower landlords as well as bosses. Imagine a domestic workers' union in the Philippines and a sex workers' collective in Mexico getting in touch to share tactics, strategy and solidarity. Imagine that the solidarity doesn't live in the campaign, but serves as a starting point for this alliance to build a vision together for a fairer workplace, community and world.

The work of aligning trade union demands with broader community, societal and global ones might at times be messy, with overlap, gaps and mismatched structures, processes and personalities to contend with. No one strategy will fit all. In de-industrialised Wales, it might be tackling unemployment that brings people together, while in inner-city London it might be exorbitant rents. It will involve trade unions, tenants' unions, community unions and students' unions. It will take workers' cooperatives; feminist, disability and faith groups; LGBT+ campaigns; racial justice movements; credit unions; charities, churches and food banks. It will require fighting back against restrictive trade union laws and the seemingly unrestricted power of capital. But it also has the potential to transform British trade unionism, halting the trend of decline and building working class alliances strong enough to take on the bosses, landlords and politicians once again.

Chapter 7

Power up: Organising in the digital age

In 1779, so the story goes, textile apprentice Ned Ludd broke into a factory and smashed a mechanised weaving machine to smithereens. The stunt afforded him hero status; 40 years on, threatened by the introduction of automated knitting frames, several more weavers and textile workers forced their way into a factory in Nottingham, sparking similar actions across the country. They called themselves the Luddites, issuing manifestos in Ned Ludd's name and pledging allegiance to 'General Ludd'. The Luddites, whose name has come to be synonymous with a general reticence towards technology, were highly skilled textile workers who feared unemployment at the hands of weaving and knitting machines operated by cheaper, unskilled workers. Such was their resistance that the army was deployed to thwart them, ultimately shooting several of their number at a Huddersfield mill when their protest did not quell. The Luddites didn't stop the advance of technology, and in fact they didn't intend to: their nuanced demands revolved far more around the control of new technologies and the fortunes of those they displaced than contemporary accounts would lead us to believe. But as fears grow about the impact of new technologies in our own lives, perhaps they have become more relatable figures. We are living through the Fourth Industrial Revolution, after all, with all the facial recognition technology, self-driving cars and humanoid robots that entails. Its full impacts remain to be seen.

What this means for workers and unions is a matter of much debate but little consensus, beyond an acceptance that its impacts will be significant. Stock phrases are rife: robots taking our jobs; our phones spying on us; our data being sold. There's a lot of heat and much less light, a lot of panic and much less understanding. But the conversations tend to take technological determinism as a starting point: an implicit acceptance of the powerlessness of individuals and collectives against the Herculean current of technological change.

'Technology always has the possibility to be a threat to any organisation and for unions that is also the case,' says Becky Wright, executive director at cross-union forum Unions 21. 'But it's not really the technology that's the problem, more so the lack of evolution and change. We have two choices: accept the advances and evolve with them, or shape those advances. If we do neither, that is the greater threat.'

Rather than being seen as an abstract and inevitable danger, perhaps our analysis of technology and work should begin from the same premise as the union movement itself: that collectively we are always strong enough to challenge and change the tides of history.

Are robots coming for our jobs?

On Valentine's Day 2016, Sophia, the world's first humanoid robot, was switched on. Able to imitate human expressions, speech and behaviour, Sophia is also built to develop over time, constantly learning from interactions how to be more and more like a human. She is a 'social robot', say her inventors, designed to develop connections with real humans and even nurture loving relationships. In her short life, Sophia has chalked up achievements most of us could never dream of, appearing at South by Southwest Festival, being appointed the United Nations' Innovation Ambassador, chatting to Jimmy Fallon on the *Tonight Show* and gracing the cover of *Elle Brasil*. But she was also designed with a much more relatable purpose in mind: to provide companionship to elderly people in care homes, or to perform tasks like crowd control at large events.[1]

It's unlikely that Sophia herself will be coming for any of our jobs, given her busy schedule of high-profile commitments – although the role of robots like her in care homes poses even more existential questions about the future of social relations and the value of care work and community. But the fear that we will be displaced or undermined by an army of increasingly intelligent and physically capable robots developed under a new wave of automation endures. Just as the invention of the lightbulb endangered the livelihood of lamplighters, and the dawn of the printing press decimated a workforce dedicated to copying books by hand, many fear that machine learning and artificial intelligence could eventually render us obsolete and usher in a new age of unemployment and limited job opportunities. And the concern isn't completely unfounded: research estimates that 30 per cent of jobs are at potential risk of automation by the mid 2030s, and that less educated workers and those in industries such as manufacturing, construction and retail are particularly at risk.[2]

---

1   https://businessinsider.com/meet-the-first-robot-citizen-sophia-animatronic-humanoid-2017-10?r=UK#a-complex-set-of-motors-and-gears-power-sophia-enabling-a-range-of-facial-expressions-3 (last accessed November 2020).

2   https://pwc.co.uk/services/economics/insights/the-impact-of-automation-on-jobs.html (last accessed November 2020).

But the evidence shows us that the true threat of new technologies in the workplace comes from how our bosses use them to fortify existing power imbalances, rather than to replace us completely. In Amazon warehouses, workers have their toilet breaks timed in a drive towards maximum efficiency over worker welfare.[3] During the 2020 Coronavirus lockdowns, a number of stories circulated about bosses rushing to monitor their workers' productivity from home through measures ranging from monitoring computer activity to the use of facial recognition technology to measure the time spent at a desk.[4] And time and again across society, we see how these technologies are leveraged against those already most marginalised, most notably people of colour: in August 2019, leaked FBI documents showed the use of a surveillance programme to monitor 'Black Identity Extremists,' understood to refer to Black Lives Matter activists.[5] Despite extensive research into racist algorithms and the ways in which technology can bolster existing biases, police surveillance cameras in the US are still disproportionately installed in Black and brown neighbourhoods.[6] Even technology which might at first appear relatively benign can be leveraged against us. When you log sick days on the HR portal at your workplace, chances are they are instantaneously plugged into a formula called the Bradford Factor, used by HR departments to measure absenteeism and predict a worker's 'risk' to the employer on the principle that short, unplanned absences are more disruptive

---

3   https://businessinsider.com/amazon-warehouse-workers-have-to-pee-into-bottles-2018-4?r=US&IR=T (last accessed November 2020).

4   https://theguardian.com/world/2020/sep/27/shirking-from-home-staff-feel-the-heat-as-bosses-ramp-up-remote-surveillance (last accessed November 2020).

5   https://aclu.org/press-releases/leaked-fbi-documents-raise-concerns-about-targeting-black-people-under-black-identi-1 (last accessed February 2021).

6   https://aclu.org/news/privacy-technology/how-is-face-recognition-surveillance-technology-racist/ (last accessed February 2021).

than long-term sick leave. You might not have known you had a Bradford Factor score; your boss probably knows what yours is.

The proliferation of app-based work, and the increasing digitisation of existing work, also presents a challenge for workers and their unions, obscuring the most basic terms of employment and complicating the relationship between bosses and workers. Deliveroo, for example, famously uses algorithms to determine both pay and the allocation of deliveries to its self-employed riders, but does not make public any details about how these algorithms operate, with the result that riders do not know how their own pay is calculated or why they are allocated the specific jobs they are given.[7] On an even more fundamental level, a number of the care workers and cleaners involved in the Glasgow Women's Strike discussed in Chapter 4 told me of the difficulties they faced in accessing their own payslips or booking leave they were entitled to since the transfer of these processes to an unreliable online system which the workers, some of them more than 30 years into their careers and nearing retirement, had not been adequately trained to use.

Of particular concern to trade unionists is the potential for technology to increase workers' sense of alienation, from the products of their labour, as per Marxist theory, but also from each other. Technology used to track and measure efficiency and productivity can create competition and erode solidarity between workers, as well as purposely separating them from one another. Algorithms used by HR departments to optimise break times, for example, are unlikely to schedule them simultaneously. Platform workers allocated shifts via an app may never even meet their colleagues in person. Where once our social connections with co-workers might have compensated

---

7   https://thebureauinvestigates.com/stories/2021-03-25/deliveroo-riders-earning-as-little-as-2-pounds (last accessed April 2021).

for the drudgery of work, now there is only drudgery. A lack of camaraderie within the workplace was cited by a number of respondents to the TUC's research into the experience of young workers – of particular concern when other challenges facing them were as basic as being paid enough to survive or having no control over their own working patterns.[8]

Clare Coatman, senior campaigner at the TUC and the person responsible for the research, says it is these bread-and-butter issues which remain central to young workers, with technology underpinning everything rather than being seen as its own distinct issue. 'When we were asking people about their challenges in the workplace, no one mentioned automation or technology,' she tells me. 'Some of the challenges that are coming up are super old; it's like Victorian piecework for the modern age.' For too long, new technology has benefitted bosses and deepened existing power imbalances, with workers reaping few of the benefits. But there are opportunities to harness its power in the project of building a strong union movement that speaks to young workers.

Technology for good

Six months after forming in April 2020, members of the Unite Registered Childminders Northern Ireland branch had still never met each other. Launching just as the Coronavirus pandemic forced the nation's citizens into their homes and onto Zoom, the predominantly female group recruited, expanded, organised and won entirely on digital platforms. Growing from no members to 300 in the space of six months, the branch communicated by video call and social media, securing virtual

---

8   https://tuc.org.uk/sites/default/files/2020-01/WorkSmart_Innovation_Project_ Report_2019_AW_Digital.pdf (last accessed November 2020).

meetings with Northern Ireland's Education and Finance Ministers, as well as party leaders, and winning a £300 increase in support grants for childminders in September, just five months into their existence.[9] In the months following, they successfully lobbied for self-isolation grants for childminders, and for these grants to be excluded from Universal Credit assessments.[10]

For experienced trade unionists familiar with the long, hard, on-the-ground graft of organising, not to mention the bureaucracy of building and registering a new branch, electing officers, and securing negotiations, the childminders' experience is nothing short of remarkable – and indeed, their story is one of brilliant grassroots organising and innovation. But for many young would-be trade unionists, the potential for relatively widespread and accessible technology to support union activity is likely self-evident. 'Half of the current workforce entered work during the internet age,' says John Wood, Digital Manager at the TUC. 'All this stuff is instinct for half the workforce; it's normal. We're not yet always meeting those expectations.'

A sluggishness by trade unions to embrace technology that does meet young workers' expectations can leave them doubly vulnerable. Subject to all the same workplace pressures and problems, young workers are just as in need of control and power at work, but potentially more likely to seek it through non-union routes that are easier to access and more in line with their other digital interactions. 'Now when people have problems they go on Change.org and start a petition,' Wood points out. 'That meets expectations, it gives them control, it fits into their lives, and

9   https://belfastlive.co.uk/news/belfast-news/education-minister-announces-300-increase-18966740?fbclid=IwAR3ezzmlkSkDUQ1ePpnvJ38usMgCgpOQoq9k1LGR cxcMaoXsf5xo5Meqd8U (last accessed April 2021).

10   https://unitelive.org/childminders-northern-ireland-form-first-ever-unite-branch/ (last accessed April 2021).

they're using the tools they want to be using. The downside is that in doing that you're cutting yourself off from collective protection, legal rights, the bigger picture.' A union-backed alternative to Change.org, an online petition site called Megaphone.org.uk, is just one innovation to have come out of Wood's Digital Lab. Since its formation, Megaphone-hosted petitions have successfully halted cuts to fire services in South Yorkshire and Devon, and forced Microsoft to remove a Microsoft 360 function which allowed managers to see individual workers' data.

There are immediate and practical steps that unions could take to meet some of these expectations and improve the experience for young members. The use of basic technology varies wildly across the movement, with fast-food workers organising via WhatsApp and Uber strikers calling for customers not to cross 'digital picket lines', while some unions still require members to join with paper forms and be formally proposed and seconded at in-person meetings. One union branch website I found in researching this book was emblazoned with WordArt and explained in a footnote that it was last updated in 1997, presumably several years before many of their youngest potential members were born. Social media, too, while no substitute on its own for deep organising, presents plenty of opportunities for unions. Meeting young people where they are, speaking in their language, and projecting an image that represents us are all vital in winning young workers back to the labour movement. The instantaneous nature of social media provides a new front on which unions can shame bad bosses and shout about their victories. Any twenty-first century union organising strategy should include employing tech-savvy communications staff familiar with the platforms on which young workers can comfortably meet, share experiences and build solidarity on their own terms.

But beyond these fundamental digital tools are also opportunities to think creatively about technology and how it might reinvigorate the very foundations of our movement. When the Broadcasting, Entertainment, Communications and Theatre Union (BECTU) teamed up with the TUC Digital Lab in 2017, they took inspiration from KickStarter, a crowdfunding platform in which no pledged donations are taken until the entire target is raised – and, ironically, a business renowned for poor employment practices and union-busting.[11] The campaign aimed to recruit an influx of new members in the Visual Effects (VFX) sector big enough to reach the threshold for official recognition. A large and fluid industry, many workers were reticent about unionisation owing to a large migrant workforce fearful about immigration status, and the project-based nature of their work which demanded finding new contracts with different employers on a regular basis. Without recognition and limited by anti-union laws, the union had little access to workplaces. But in partnership with the TUC, they built a Kickstarter-style tool which presented a target number of new members and gave workers the option of joining immediately, or pledging to join only when that target was reached. Over the course of a month, 28 per cent of joiners opted to sign up on the spot, with 72 per cent committing to join if the goal was recognised.[12]

This use of new digital tools to meet the most fundamental of union challenges – a fear of retribution, a slog to reach the threshold for recognition – is all the more satisfying for its turning of the inventions of the big tech, boss class against itself. The developments we instinctively fear can either be the ruin

11 https://bbc.com/news/world-us-canada-49692983 (last accessed November 2020).

12 https://digital.tuc.org.uk/kick-starting-the-union-bectu-vfx-recruitment-pilot/ (last accessed November 2020).

or the making of us. Widespread panic about big data and the misuse of our personal information grips the world, and is a legitimate cause in a society structured to bolster the power of bosses. But it is not data itself that is inherently bad. In fact, it is data that allows us to see the existence of pay gaps, or the impact of outsourcing on wages, and it is data that could allow us to map global chains of exploitation, tracking the lifetime of an iPhone from Silicon Valley designer to Chinese factory worker to Apple Store retailer to Hermes delivery driver. If the advance of technology is inevitable, it falls to the union movement to ensure it is our weapon as much as it is the weapon of our bosses.

Organising digital workplaces

In 2019, American RideShare driver and YouTuber 'Dustin is Driving' uploaded an eight-minute long video entitled 'Uber- I Can't Beleive [sic] Drivers Admitted To Doing "Surge Club"',[13] complete with hashtags #uberscams, #uber and #lyft. In the clip, he referred to a long-standing practice in which platform-based drivers can generate surge prices by simultaneously switching their apps off and on again. Reading from news reports, Dustin described Uber and Lyft drivers at Reagan National Airport, Virginia, coordinating to carry out the practice several times a night, every night, in an act of resistance against the low wages paid out by bosses making their millions. A driver employed via an app, using a smartphone to film himself, discussing digital resistance tactics, on a YouTube channel, is two things: the perfect tableau of our digital age, and a call to action for unions to ensure their strategies and tactics are as effective in digital workplaces as they have been on the factory floor.

---

13 https://youtube.com/watch?v=SYkLhXMsZ8I (last accessed November 2020).

The new media sector, in the USA and closer to home, is so far proving this to be true. Since the spring of 2015, over 60 digital and legacy publications have unionised,[14] just as concerns have grown about the influence of publishers like Facebook and the proliferation of online advertising. There are key factors driving the surge for unionisation across the sector: mergers and layoffs as news sites struggle to compete; a 'pivot to video' driven by changes to the Facebook algorithm which displaced journalists and restructured teams; the monopolisation of advertising revenue by omnipresent tech companies. The challenges might be new but, as a whole generation of journalists and creatives have discovered, the answers are old: collective action and solidarity in the face of competition and atomisation.

In the tech industry itself, workers occupy a unique position as both the producers of technology which threatens us, and the victims of those threats. Employed by some of the biggest bosses in the world – including in the 'big 4' tech companies Apple, Amazon, Facebook and Google – they simultaneously build, maintain and operate the code, machines and algorithms that are used against us, while also being at the mercy of billionaires with unrestrained power and wealth, whose sole interests look to be shoring up more of it. But even here, unions are beginning to gain ground. The tech industry represents 9 per cent of the workforce in the UK,[15] but has so far been almost entirely unorganised, until 2020 when the Communications Workers Union (CWU) welcomed a new branch, the United Tech and Allied Workers (UTAW), made up of workers from across companies like Google, Microsoft, Monzo and Apple. Some of their causes are bread and butter union issues – insecure contracts at Monzo;

14   Nicole S. Cohen and Greig de Peuter, *New Media Unions: Organising Digital Journalists* (London: Routledge, 2020) pp. 1–3.
15   https://wired.co.uk/article/united-tech-and-allied-workers-union (last accessed November 2020).

unfair dismissal at Google – but some are unique to their place in companies that dominate the stock market, halls of power, and our everyday lives. As the processing of our personal data increasingly generates profits for private companies, for example, should we be compensated for the work of providing it? Can tech unions spearhead a movement for data unionisation and democratic ownership of data that aligns the interests of workers and citizens across the world? Across the country, unions are proving that they can work in digital workplaces and against big tech. The age-old principles of collectivism and building working class power stand steadfast against novel challenges like clickbait, data rights and the platform economy – and ever-present ones like excessive profits and job insecurity.

Sharing technology's benefits means not just wresting back its power from our bosses but also acknowledging the harms of digital colonialism. Any union serious about leveraging technology in their work must think deeply about how advanced technology in the Global North often thrives on the marginalisation of our counterparts in the Global South, where the concentration of tech factories and sweatshops provides a stark contrast to Silicon Valley HQs, and where vast swathes of the population are either locked out of accessing technologies or entirely at the mercy of Western tech giants to do so. In 2017, for example, Facebook launched its Free Basics internet service for 'developing markets' in countries including Colombia, Ghana and Pakistan, but was accused of not adequately serving local populations and harvesting huge amounts of metadata in a violation of net neutrality (the principle that Internet Service Providers should treat all communications equally and without discrimination).[16] To think about global solidarity in the context

---

16   https://advox.globalvoices.org/2017/07/27/can-facebook-connect-the-next-billion/ (last accessed February 2021).

of technology is difficult, thorny work where little has been done yet, but it is incumbent on unions to consider these challenges as they incorporate new technologies in their organising.

It could be tempting to answer the double-pronged challenge of attracting young workers and embracing technology with blunt instruments and easy answers: a laptop discount when you sign up; a Twitter account firing out one liners and sassy gifs; a one-stop-shop union app. Certainly, these developments would be welcome. But it would be a mistake to see them as the only, or indeed the most vital, ways of adapting to new technologies or recruiting new members. It is, as it always has been, political education, deep organising and visible wins that create new trade unionists. Just look at the University and College Union (UCU), who saw a 16 per cent increase in members in a year, following twelve months of strike action over pensions.[17] Rather, developments in technology can help us to deliver that political education, carry out that deep organising, and communicate those visible wins we achieve as a result. Not to embrace them in our work is to forego a whole swathe of potential new organising tools and settings.

The most urgent questions for the union movement, then, are not about how we guard our jobs against robots or halt the tides of change, but about how we fight to make technology work for us and not against us. Can we organise for worker and community ownership of the technology that will one day rule the world? Can we expand the scope of collective bargaining to cover the introduction of new technologies in the workplace? Can we turn the tools of our bosses into the tools of our organising? Can we use our skills, experience and strategies to build solidarity in digital workplaces? Or reap the benefits of automa-

---

17   https://tes.com/news/strike-action-boosts-ucu-membership (last accessed November 2020).

tion with a four-day week, some form of Universal Basic Income or Services,[18] and a recalibration of the dominance of work in our lives? A united working class has changed the course of history before, and the relentless march of technology provides an opportunity for it to do so again.

---

18 'Universal Basic Income' is one of many terms for a concept which can take different forms, but which ultimately refers to regular payments from the state to its citizens without means testing or eligibility criteria. 'Universal Basic Services' refers to the free, unconditional provision of basic public services such as transport, housing and internet access from the state to its citizens.

Chapter 8

Reimagining union democracy

When 29-year-old Esme Stevens[1] started organising the call centre she worked at, she quickly caught the union bug. Grafting hard in an unrecognised workplace and fresh from completing a Masters degree in social research, she had hoped to combine her academic background with her organising experience to help her union better understand unrecognised workplaces and improve its offer to workers within them. When she visited the union's head office on a different matter, she asked for directions to the research department and made her way upstairs.

'I didn't really feel like I was meant to be there,' says Stevens of head office. The staff member she found in the research office 'just seemed a bit baffled' to see her. He talked her through some current research projects and gave her a report on organising strategies, suggesting she read it and email back her thoughts. 'There was loads of great stuff in there but I didn't feel like I could hear the voices of our members in it,' she says of the report. 'I emailed him quite detailed feedback identifying this gap in the research.' He never replied to the email.

If we are to move away from outdated rhetoric which situates 'the union' as an abstract entity, and move towards an understanding of unions as workers and workers as unions, then

---

1   Not her real last name.

harnessing and cultivating Esme's skills, on-the-ground experience and enthusiasm to this end appears to be a no-brainer. The evidence also says so. In research about the untapped potential of new members, Kurt Vandaele of the European Trade Union Institute outlines how most members who leave the union do so in the early years of their membership, and how new, young members bring with them creativity and fresh ideas unhampered by previous experiences.[2] But perhaps even more importantly, the very values on which the union movement was founded say so too: what is the point of a union if not to build power among its rank and file members?

As unions have become larger, older and more institutionalised, the central functions of many have become increasingly alienated from the workers they serve. Mergers have created a number of sprawling, generalist super-unions which necessitate layers of hierarchy and bureaucracy, and account for the majority of union members. Meanwhile, small and specialist unions continue to benefit from their strong identities but often lack the resources and expertise to organise effectively. Some unions represent a craft – that is, a specific job role – while others organise whole industries. Some are centuries old with buildings full of staff and policies printed on a typewriter, while others have existed for less than a decade and run on a shoestring budget. Affiliation to the TUC or other umbrella bodies adds an extra layer of union democracy for members to navigate. And it is this culture of labyrinthine and stale democracy, underpinned by the erosion of union rights, that has seen some corners of the movement slide into conservative hegemony, with a fear of or unwillingness to act rebelliously and boldly spawning alle-

---

2   https://unions21.org.uk/ideas/trade-union-newcomers-an-untapped-resource (last accessed November 2020).

gations of no-strike agreements,[3] accusations of government pandering and the growing division between 'establishment' and 'grassroots' unions from the left. In trying to map the structure of the UK-wide trade union movement, a sprawling network akin to a detective's wall of push pins and thread spreads out in front of us.

The effect of this maelstrom for a new, uninitiated trade unionist is a perception that union democracy and culture is impenetrable, alienating and fundamentally broken, and while that's not a universal truth, it's not altogether incorrect either. Our democracy was built in the image of a movement and a labour market that have changed beyond all recognition; a failure to evolve with those changes has left unions in competition with each other for members, resources and political influence, in an identity crisis over their relationship to the Labour Party, and in some cases focussed on managing their own decline rather than adapting and rejuvenating. But new forms of democracy which reimagine leadership, empower rank-and-file members and reconsider our parliamentary influence are within our reach.

In referring to union democracy I take the term in its widest sense, as encompassing macro structures of representation, leadership and electoral politics, but also the everyday mechanisms of union membership, communications and operations on the ground in individual workplaces. Thinking in these terms allows us to identify barriers to participation that might feel insurmountable in their institutionalisation, but which can certainly be worked through and overcome.

For example, membership rates can be prohibitive to young and particularly precarious workers: can we introduce a 'pay what you can' rate based in trust, or a rate calculated on weekly shifts

---

3   https://employmentwrites.com/2020/01/26/gmbs-no-strike-agreement/ (last accessed February 2021).

rather than monthly wages? The requirement for a specified period of membership before being able to access union support is similarly exclusionary for young workers in the 2020s, who could lose their job and livelihood while running down the clock on their membership. Can we build a rapid response structure that kicks in immediately and then moves new members into the union structures proper? And the question of which union to join is complicated enough without considering that many young workers change jobs and employers regularly. Can we build a union passport that allows young workers to move seamlessly through our structures and ensures that when we create new members, we don't lose them again in a year?

Similarly, we must develop new mechanisms for measuring our own success. Union density measures can tell us the share of employees in an industry or workplace that are members of a trade union, but says nothing about their levels of engagement or their union's activity or effectiveness within that workplace. Can we embed in our structures the ability to take the temperature of our organising, rather than just checking for its pulse?

While many unions had already begun to think through some of these nuts-and-bolts challenges, the Coronavirus pandemic undoubtedly forced them to act fast and update some of the most basic elements of their democracy almost overnight. In one example, ASLEF, the train drivers' union, found themselves having to establish all-member bulletins and surveys for the first time, when nationalisation of the railways meant that negotiations took place between all unions and government at once, and any decisions taken applied across the sector rather than to one operator. To think anew about union democracy must be to include these most basic of operations while also embracing bigger-scale innovation and experiment.

A political voice?

On 25 June 2020, in response to Labour leader Keir Starmer's sacking of shadow education minister Rebecca Long-Bailey, political journalist Paul Waugh tweeted: 'Starmer's choice as new shadow education secretary will be interesting. Some Lab [sic] MPs felt Long-Bailey too often sounded like the parliamentary wing of the National Education Union, rather than an advocate for parents, teachers and pupils.'[4]

A tweet is 280 characters long and Waugh didn't even use all of them. But in hitting send, he managed to neatly encapsulate at least three contemporary confusions around the link between unions and the parliamentary Labour Party. Why should the interests of a teachers' union and those of parents, teachers and pupils always be in opposition? Why shouldn't a shadow cabinet minister in the party founded to be the parliamentary wing of the unions sound like the parliamentary wing of the unions? And why would it be Labour MPs complaining about that?

The trade union movement and its parliamentary counterpart have both evolved drastically since their respective formations, with the result being a confused and often fraught relationship between the two. But a relationship there is. As previously mentioned, the unions founded the Labour Party at the turn of the twentieth century to give the labour movement representation and influence at state level. Links between political parties and the labour movement exist in other countries, but none as institutionalised as in the UK, where a specific body (The Trade Union & Labour Party Liaison Organisation) operates to oversee the relationship, and where members of affiliated trade unions

---

4   https://twitter.com/paulwaugh/status/1276156851621593088?s=21&fbclid=Iw AR3qywCuuJto-kWtGgCMBhaBGa63QrziaHVfi9RbOQXr8knMjSl8pp2YYvA (last accessed November 2020).

have historically been automatically enrolled as party members. For a time, when the labour movement and parliamentary party could effectively operate as two sides of the same coin, this alliance was a force to be reckoned with.

But now, as uncomfortable a truth as it is for both sides, the same link comes up often when I talk to young workers about their reticence to join a union, or with organisers about the barriers they face in recruiting them. Antipathy towards the Labour Party is particularly strong both among a generation of young people who feel sold out and unrepresented by the party's shift rightwards, and within certain geographical areas where people have seen that shift in action. In Scotland, for example, where pro-independence parties enjoy a parliamentary majority and where the 2014 independence referendum politicised a generation, many young people cannot fathom automatic and non-consultative support for a party that campaigned alongside the Tories for what they see as a regressive union. A relationship that once existed to give democratic legitimacy to the union movement now looks, to many, wholly undemocratic.

For all the gripes from right-wing Labour members and the party's opponents about 'union barons' and the unwieldy influence of the unions on the party, it is the unions who have least to gain from the relationship. The party enjoys boosted membership numbers, an active base and financial gains, while the union movement reaps a political voice stuck endorsing neo-liberalism from the opposition benches. Meanwhile, it's still the parliamentary project that many on the left plough their efforts into, seeing success at the ballot box as an end in itself rather than the establishment of a working-class voice at state level. Clearly, the mechanisms of the link between the unions and the Labour party is one element of union democracy that requires fresh thinking if we are to attract a new generation of trade unionists. But the real questions are about how we can leverage our power within the Labour party as we do within our workplaces, and how we might support the advancement of a labour movement voice within electoral structures, without that voice being watered down in the process. Power, after all, is built by collectivism, not gifted by a presiding officer.

The election of Keir Starmer as leader in 2020 heralded a new conversation about these links, with unions including the Bakers, Food and Allied Workers Union announcing their intention to consult members on the possibility of disaffiliation. This decision is a strategic one on which unions and their members will come down on different sides, but those who choose to stay will likely make most progress by viewing the Labour Party as just another site on which to organise as we do in our workplaces. Such unions will certainly find a role for themselves in holding Starmer to account on his promise to work with the labour movement, and in pursuing broad-based and pragmatic agendas to the benefit of the working class, as seen, for example, in the generally non-partisan call for increased sick pay during the Coronavirus pandemic. But as with unions themselves, restrictive structures make progress difficult: anyone committed to changing the party from within may find their time best spent organising around its own internal structures and processes, pushing for institutional change.

The leadership paradox

Unions are full of contradictions. They exist to challenge capitalist relations but do so within the frameworks built by capitalism. They rail against power differentials while running on hierarchy. And they champion the interests of ordinary workers by plucking some out of the very workplaces they represent; that is, to become full-time union-employed officers. Some degree of contradiction might be inevitable under capitalism, but some might be resisted if we are prepared to think differently and imaginatively. While democratic structures vary from union to union, most take as their basic framework a hierarchy with leaders at the top and a network of 'local' (be it geographical or workplace) representatives beneath them. These roles are often elected in a process which perpetuates internal inequalities, with candidates making promises to, for example, a well-organised factory of several hundred workers representing several hundred votes rather than an unrecognised shop or bar representing ten. Union leaders and representatives, then, occupy a contradictory space; simultaneously *of* the workers, beholden *to* the workers, and with power *over* the workers.

'There is a fundamental change in material interests when someone becomes a paid member of union staff,' says Jamie Woodcock, an academic researching labour organising at the Open University. 'Union officials want to negotiate a deal, and they often want to get people back to work, so they're prepared to settle for a lot less. They're always tied between representing members and making sure the union continues going along.'

Often, we channel our frustrations about the dynamic Woodcock describes into criticisms of 'union bureaucrats' or 'middle managers' of the type encountered by Esme Stevens. Certainly, both exist; it is undeniable that there are those who have entered union structures to secure a job for life, and therefore have a vested interest in the status quo and an inherent conflict with rank-and-file members. But more interesting is the way in which union structures can require any one of us to develop these same interests and engage in these same conflicts when we step into them. In this context, the reimagining of union democracy demands that we ask: how can we hold unions and representatives to account and ensure that they listen to their members? How can union structures produce an equilibrium between leaders obliged by conservatism and members demanding militancy? What does a democratic unionism look like?

As a starting point, we might look further afield, firstly to arguably the biggest union in the world, America's Teamsters. While the national roles of General President and General Secretary-Treasurer still exist, a decentralised structure means they are supported by 22 vice presidents located regionally or at large, and by three trustees appointed to hold the organisation accountable on its expenditure. At a local level, branches are largely autonomous and keep their own membership dues, elect their own officers, and vote on their own structures and policies, with members therefore benefitting from both a strong voice at local level and the institutional backing of a nationwide union. The Teamsters highlight the possibility of a structure which generates more meaningful engagement without deviating too far from traditional union set-ups – but there are possibilities to think even bigger, too.

The future of union democracy

In June 2020, eight months after the World Health Organisation declared the COVID-19 pandemic an international public health emergency, the Centre for Economic Policy Research and the World Economic Forum co-published a report entitled 'Leading the Fight Against the Pandemic: Does Gender "Really" Matter?'[5] Stepping into a debate that had long rumbled among the public, the authors sought to map COVID-19 outcomes against coun-

---

5   https://papers.ssrn.com/sol3/papers.cfm?abstract_id=3617953   (last   accessed November 2020).

tries with female leadership in order to systematically scrutinise the widespread assertion that they performed better. And it was true, they found, that women-led countries saw more effective pandemic responses. Time and again, outcomes like these are attributed to the individual and supposedly innate qualities of women leaders. Perhaps we're just more caring and compassionate, or our experiences of motherhood uniquely equip us to parent a country? Or maybe it's that women are socially conditioned to be patient, conciliatory and able to keep multiple plates spinning at once?

Aside from its essentialist and reductionist view of womanhood, this is also a position that sacrifices analysis of structures and systems in favour of dissecting the qualities of individual women. If we were to dig a little deeper, we would find that the countries most likely to elect women leaders are also those with democratic structures and electoral systems that encourage a more consensual style of leadership and decision-making than their hierarchical and autocratic counterparts. In other words, successful women leaders might be the products of better governance rather than the architects of it.

It's little coincidence, then, that the Labour Party, with its structures replicated from those of the trade union movement, has, at the time of writing, never elected a woman leader, or that women leaders are still a minority in the movement despite making up the majority of its membership. As discussed in Chapter 4, unions are built in the image of a white, male breadwinner, with all the traditional, top-down, masculine-coded leadership that implies and the democratic structures that have allowed it to prevail.

'The structures are so reflective of conservative with a small "c" politics,' says Bryan Simpson, industrial organiser with Unite.

People who hold onto power, unyielding power. Conveners who've been there for thirty years who don't like young women coming through telling them what to do. If we fixed our structures, all of the obstacles of accessibility, diversity . . . I can't see any of the logistical obstacles not just being instantly moved. That's the number one thing to change.

To build a liberatory, fighting union movement fit for the future must be to think differently about that movement's structures.

While the labour movement largely operates on a system of hierarchical leadership, its comrades in the workers' cooperative movement have tended to build their structures around its opposite, social leadership. Spain's Mondragon, the largest cooperative in the world, uses general assemblies to appoint managers, for example, and includes in its structures 'social councils', explicitly designed to balance managerial direction with members' concerns. Rather than a pyramid structure with power gifted from top-to-bottom at the behest of a uniquely influential few, social leadership implies consensual and communal decision-making, with leaders earning their position through ongoing mutual respect rather than short-lived oppositional contests. Social leadership, which necessitates acknowledgement of the rank-and-file in any organisation's success, may therefore have far more in common with union values than the hierarchal structures we currently share with our bosses.

There are countless ways in which unions could begin to embody social leadership, and hardly any of them require tearing down the entire framework and starting from scratch. It could be in co-producing an organising strategy with rank-and-file members, or in operating some form of union citizens' assembly or jury service as part of decision-making. It might be in adapting participatory budgeting for the labour movement, or mandating a certain amount of a general secretary's time spent within different union branches. It might be all of these things or something else entirely, but however it looks, embracing it will serve to redistribute power throughout the movement and truly listen to members, solving a great many problems in the process and allowing us to enact our principles of collectivism and power-building.

The structures in which we operate dictate our culture and every element of our struggles, victories and defeats. It is vital that they are fit for purpose. A truly democratic trade unionism means one which is easy to understand, access and navigate, and which has the mechanisms to measure and reckon with its own successes and shortcomings. It means one which is radical in its understandings of leadership and democracy, building grassroots power through structures which embody its values from the ground up. If our movement is to be rebuilt for a new generation, we must be prepared to reimagine what we consider fundamental, and to make fundamental what we imagine.

Chapter 9

Organising hospitality:
A toolkit for the future

It is Thursday 4 October 2018 and, in the USA, Belgium, Italy, Germany, Japan and the Philippines, fast-food workers have downed tools and taken to the streets. In the UK, strikers from McDonald's and Wetherspoons, backed by the Bakers Food and Allied Workers Union (BFAWU), are joined by Unite members from TGI Fridays, and by UberEats and Deliveroo drivers organised by the IWGB, IWW, and the GMB. The workers are united in their demands: a £10 an hour wage; an end to precarious contacts; a right to union recognition. The Twitter hashtags #McStrike, #SpoonStrike, #AllEyesOnTGIs and #FFS410 (Fast-Food Shutdown 4/10) trend continuously throughout the day. The protests – marches; rallies; parties; tweets – begin at midnight and don't wrap up until nearly 24 hours later.

In the chapters preceding, we have explored how unions and organisers are evolving to meet the needs of young workers, and imagined how young workers themselves might continue to shape the movement from the inside. There is no silver bullet, one-stop shop or perfect blueprint for this project: every worker, sector, union and campaign will necessarily look different. But there are lessons and tools we can utilise, and places we can find them. In hospitality, the biggest employer of young workers in the UK[1] and one of the most insecure sectors, a quiet revolution is underway. New branches and longstanding unions are working together to organise brand new workplaces, an uncompromising liberatory unionism, and the building of alliances both local and global on issues beyond the workplace. Organisers and members have embraced new technology, brought fresh thinking to union structures, and used unions as a training ground in the politicisation of a whole generation of waitresses, barmen, receptionists and chefs. How have they done it and what can we learn from them?

Organising precarious workers

It is Tuesday 24 November 2020 and outside the Lanyon Building, Queen's University Belfast, activists wearing face masks and standing six feet apart have just unfurled a banner reading 'Zero hours zero pay: hospitality workers demand respect.' Backed by Unite Hospitality, they are protesting the University's decision to close the students' union bar during a second Coronavirus lockdown without re-furloughing the zero-hour workers there, a situation which Unite says has left some unable to pay rent and with concerns about the future of their studies. A student with a megaphone leads the chant: 'hey hey, ho ho, put us back on furlough'. Red Unite flags wave in the foreground; behind them, imposing metal gates emblazoned with 'Queen's University Belfast' remain closed. But three weeks later, the University will reverse on their decision and place the workers on 100 per cent furlough following huge public support for the union's action.

---

1   https://tuc.org.uk/sites/default/files/2020-06/Young%20workers%20and%20
at%20risk%20industries%20-%20research%20note%20-%20final%20draft.pdf
(last accessed November 2020).

Zero-hour contracts and insecure arrangements dominate the hospitality industry, with employers often leveraging the youth of their workforce as justification for their use: students prefer the flexibility; young people are just working for beer money and not survival. But as the Queen's University protestors highlighted, that's rarely true. Young workers come in all shapes and sizes – they might be parents or students or both, supported financially by family or not, with savings or without. In reality, a great many young workers find themselves at the sharp end of insecurity and precarity, and alone in a sector that the labour movement has been reluctant to enter.

Unite Hospitality was established in 2017 to change that. With roots in Scotland, it now has offshoots in all nations of the UK, and a country-wide Fair Hospitality charter[2] that calls for a living wage, equal pay, fair tips and union access, among other demands. Building this coverage has meant taking the risk of devoting resources to unorganised sectors and workers who are not yet union members, as well as thinking differently about traditional union activity. Bryan Simpson, Unite's only full-time organiser for hospitality, can often be found calling out businesses on social media and supporting workers to organise direct actions. His approach is clear: when a single worker arrives with a grievance, the union works with them to collectivise the issue and recruit other co-workers who can then fight as a united group. The victory, or the process of working for it, creates a de-facto union branch strong enough to advance the Fair Hospitality Charter in their workplace and secure trade union recognition, building collective bargaining coverage across a sector characterised by precarious work.

That approach has paid off. 'We're a trade union unlike any other,' says Simpson. 'We're the only bespoke campaign for hos-

---

2   https://fairhospitality.org/ (last accessed November 2020).

pitality workers which is actually resourcing equality, equal pay campaigns, sexual harassment campaigns, fair tips campaigns. We're speaking in the language of hospitality workers because it's not me putting it together, it's them. And we're winning – we're moving employers towards collective bargaining agreements that set standards for the industry'.

A liberatory unionism

It is Tuesday 18 September 2018 and McDonald's workers in more than ten cities across the USA have walked off the job in what they have branded their own '#MeToo moment'. The first time that workers at the fast-food chain have taken strike action over sexual harassment, they are backed by the Time's Up campaign, founded by Hollywood celebrities in the aftermath of the Harvey Weinstein scandal, and by Fight for 15, the workers' movement organising for a living wage in the fast-food sector. Slogans in English and Spanish adorn colourful placards in Los Angeles[3] and Black women from Missouri to Florida deliver powerful speeches recounting the racialised harassment they have received at work. They don't know it yet, but in a year's time, the company's CEO Steve Easterbrook will be sacked when his relationship with an employee is revealed.[4]

The fast-food industry in both the USA and the UK is dominated by women, and disproportionately employs migrants and people of colour.[5] These workers know that their social

3 https://commondreams.org/news/2018/09/18/metoo-movement-takes-mcdonalds-workers-strike-against-sexual-harassment-epidemic (last accessed November 2020).

4 https://nytimes.com/2019/11/03/business/mcdonalds-ceo-fired-steve-easterbrook.html (last accessed November 2020).

5 https://people1st.co.uk/getattachment/Insight-opinion/Latest-insights/Industry-profiles/Hospitality-tourism-skills-and-workforce-profile-2016.pdf/?lang=en-GB&lang=en-GB (last accessed November 2020).

identity shapes their working lives, and vice versa. A 2018 survey by Unite found that 90 per cent of hospitality workers in the UK had experienced sexual harassment in the course of their job, while a lawsuit filed by 52 Black McDonald's franchisees in the US in 2020 alleged systematic racial discrimination – the third that year to do so.

Rather than shoehorning these workers and their experiences into a structure designed for white men, hospitality's women of colour and other marginalised workers have taken their place at the core of their unions' work and fought for industrial strategies and tactics that account for the interdependence between class and other forms of marginalisation. In St. Louis, Missouri, on that day in October 2018, male workers chanted along and cheered as Black women led the chant: 'Hold the burgers, hold the fries, keep your hands off my thighs'.[6]

In the UK, 2020 saw Sarah Woolley elected as the BFAWU's first ever woman general secretary, just over a year after the union launched a campaign in partnership with Women Against Rape that sought to explicitly draw a line between sexual harassment at work and austerity, social housing and the welfare system. Inspired by their American counterparts, the Bakers' Union sought to create a #MeToo moment that spoke to low-paid fast-food workers as much as Hollywood actresses. A woman of colour harassed at a McDonald's counter knows that her race, gender and job are indivisible in her experience; now, organised hospitality workers are forcing the movement to recognise that too.

Transcending the workplace

It is Monday 1 August 2016 and trade unionists have gathered outside the London Holborn branch of Byron Burgers. They have rallied from

6   https://nbcnews.com/news/us-news/mcdonald-s-workers-go-strike-over-sexual-harassment-n910656 (November 2020).

across the city, and from unions including the Industrial Workers of the World (IWW), Unite Hotel Workers Branch and United Voices of the World (UVW), as well as protest and community groups like War on Want, the Anti-Raids Network, London Latinxs and Lesbians and Gays Support the Miners (LGSM). Just over a week earlier, Byron – part of a chain owned by the private equity fund Hutton Collins Partners – invited a number of their migrant workers to 15 special 'training sessions' in restaurants across London where they were met by immigration police who detained at least 35 workers, going on to deport 25.[7] In Holborn, banners take aim at both Byron Burgers and the UK Home Office and Border Agency. Veteran trade unionists chant and sing alongside young, queer, migrant activists.

Like all workers, those in hospitality are also citizens, parents, renters, community members, friends, carers and voters. Across the sector, unions have successfully managed to align the interests of their members with those of the wider community and society, moving beyond workplace and geographical parochialism and building alliances that advance the working class as a whole.

Many workers in hospitality, and in precarious work generally, are also migrants. When unions mobilised in response to Byron's immigration sting, they recognised immediately that their opponents were an alliance of powerful forces, working in cooperation to protect their shared interests: bosses and governments, profits and borders. Responding as a single workforce from a single workplace wouldn't cut it; the response needed to be as multi-faceted as the attack.

In Scotland, the Better than Zero campaign for precarious workers has built a strong partnership with tenants' union Living Rent in an attempt to take back control of labour, land

---

7 https://theguardian.com/uk-news/2016/aug/01/byron-burger-chain-asks-protesters-to-respect-customers-safety (last accessed November 2020).

and housing, understood by the unions as interconnected issues that affect each of their members at once. Likewise, the BFAWU have set an example for the rest of the union movement through their work on climate justice, including joining school pupils on climate strikes, becoming only the second union to call for a general strike on climate change, and successfully proposing a historic TUC policy to back the nationalisation and democratisation of the energy sector.

Hospitality unions understand better than many that the issues facing their members go beyond the workplace, and that working-class power is built through local and global alliances. Whether it's synchronising action with American workers, leveraging union power behind urgent societal issues, or creating coherent narratives about exploitation that span work, housing and welfare, hospitality unions are working to transcend individual workplaces and build power with a base broad enough to take on capital in all its forms.

Organising in the digital age

It is Tuesday 24 March 2020 and Wetherspoons chairman Tim Martin has just sent a video message to his employees telling them they will be paid late. The government has announced its furlough scheme: 80 per cent of wages up to the value of £2,500 a month for those whose jobs are unsustainable during the Coronavirus lockdown. But Martin won't pay staff until that money is made available, which could take a month – and he suggests they get a job in Tesco in the meantime.[8] The BFAWU spring into action; by the end of the evening, more than 800 Wetherspoons workers are organised into WhatsApp groups ready to fight back. The next day Tim Martin will cave and commit to a partial U-turn, agreeing to front the 80 per cent wages until

---

8   https://bbc.co.uk/news/business-52018360 (last accessed November 2020).

the government money is available. But the BFAWU will be ready, refusing to let the moment slide: a petition on the TUC's Megaphone platform will call for Wetherspoons to pay the remaining 20 per cent and 14,500 people will sign it.[9]

The precarious and shift-based nature of hospitality work makes traditional organising difficult in bars, restaurants and hotels. In place of branch meetings and paper forms, hospitality unions have increasingly built solidarity on hashtags, WhatsApp groups and websites, making use of new technologies to bolster organising rather than replacing it. That Martin backed down in under 24 hours speaks to a digital organising strategy that engendered instant resistance: mobilising those affected, spreading the word, instigating a public backlash too powerful to ignore, and all in less than a day.

UK workers can also take inspiration from their Australian counterparts, who were the first in the world to launch a digital union for hospitality workers. Hospo Voice, part of the United Voice union, one of Australia's largest, provides all union services online for the cost of a Spotify subscription, as well as using their technological foundations to build new organising tools. Members can 'Rate [Their] Boss', submitting reviews to warn others of problem employers, as well as making use of sexual harassment diaries, a pay checker to calculate correct pay rates, and a time checker to log shifts.

This division of the labour movement originated in bakeries and butchers' shops, but is today defined by a young workforce increasingly having to contend with apps, self-service machines and precarious contracts that make physical solidarity increasingly impossible. But unions are adapting to this reality, making use of digital tools to support their organising, overcoming the

9   https://megaphone.org.uk/petitions/email-wetherspoons-to-demand-they-pay-workers-laid-off-during-Coronavirus (last accessed November 2020).

erosion of solidarity with new spaces in which to build it, and using new methods to ensure the tried and tested ones are as strong as ever.

Reimagining union democracy

It is a dark December evening in 2018 and more than 20 young bar and restaurant workers, most of them women, are crowded around a table in a pub in Stirling, Scotland. Unite Hospitality have paid for some drinks and snacks but these workers organised themselves, more than 50 of them unhappy with their treatment and conditions in one of Scotland's most concentrated hospitality sectors. They meet on a Monday evening, because Saturday afternoon meetings don't work for hospitality. They avoid the word 'branch', because jargon might put off potential new members. They tell Unite they need childcare to make meetings accessible to parents. They tell Unite how they want to run their meetings. A year later they will have 350 members, be a fully constituted branch of Unite, and still retain control over their own campaigns and processes.

With a blank slate and on a mission to reach a whole new sector of primarily young, primarily non-union savvy workers, Unite Hospitality has been able to think differently about what a progressive union structure looks like. Where practical barriers have emerged, they have been removed: a zero-hour membership rate was introduced when dues were too high for precarious workers, and organisers have changed their working day to account for late-evening meetings that accommodate hospitality shifts. Speed of response is essential for precarious workers living pay cheque to pay cheque, so organisers like Simpson routinely forego the four-week membership period traditionally required for workers to access union support, instead making a deal: I'll put my neck on the line to help you immediately, if you put the work in to unionise more of your co-workers.

These changes have been made immediately and with ease because Unite Hospitality is able to operate on a form of social leadership rather than hierarchy. Groups of workers retain control over their own campaigns and organising strategies, at different times instructing and seeking support from organisers. In hospitality, unions are listening to their young workers, putting their ideas into action, and winning as a result.

* * *

I don't highlight hospitality organising here to suggest that organising in this sector has been perfected, but I highlight the tactics and strategies employed there because they are instructional. In the preceding chapters I have asked questions of the labour movement, challenging us to think creatively, sometimes about some of our most fundamental beliefs. I have presented a vision of a radically different movement and, it might seem, asked you to take a leap of faith in believing that it could work. I present these examples from hospitality and, throughout this book, from others in the union movement already embracing new modes of organising, to illustrate that the leap is not so big; that it is within our power to break into unorganised sectors, prioritise liberatory politics, campaign beyond our workplaces, embrace new technologies, reimagine union structures and act as a training ground for the young working class. To do so will be the making of our movement for a whole new generation.

Conclusion: How unions change our lives

If there is one lesson that you take from this book, I hope it is that collective action is what changes the world. Perhaps you didn't know a lot about unions, didn't think they were for you, didn't think they were powerful, or didn't believe they were fit for purpose in the current day. I hope I have dispelled some of those notions in these pages, but more than that I hope I have shown that the answers to them are ours to decide. There is no abstract, unknowable 'union'; no finite, locked box of power; no inevitable conclusion. There is only you, and me, and us, and what we choose to do.

I have tried to set out a vision of the unionism a new generation could build if we rose to that challenge. A unionism that takes the best of the labour movement's traditions and the bold, innovative organising it continues to inspire. One that builds intergenerational, liberatory and global solidarity. One that embraces new and radical thinking, and is at the forefront of building a strong and united working class that speaks to the age we live in. We need unions, for their protection, for their power, for their principles, and they need us, to lead this change and ensure they will still be fighting when a new generation follows.

I began this book by recounting my own union journey. Having gone on to explore the role of unions in workplaces, class relations and society at large, it feels fitting to close by once again emphasising the profound role they can have in our own lives. My life, work, ideology and many of my most meaningful relationships have been shaped by the things I have learned from, in, and about unions. Almost every organiser I spoke to for this book told me countless similar stories, about people whose self-belief, outlook or life course changed as a result of union membership. Many sentiments came up again and again: they didn't know how good they were; they took some convincing but now they're formidable; they've made friends for life through their organising. Anny Cullum, organiser with community union ACORN, highlighted the transformative impact unions can have on their members when she recounted the following experience:

> When I was [a local] organiser we recruited someone, and I got her to stand for a position in the local neighbourhood's branch. She did an amazing job but she was so nervous. Now, she's just developed and developed through her work with us, and now she's chair of the whole [city] branch. She'd never really done anything like this before, and the other day we were talking about job interviews and she said to me: 'you know when you grow up on the poverty line, you always have this imposter syndrome when you go to job interviews? I think ACORN's helped beat some of that out of me because I've shown myself that I can do stuff.'

It would be easy to celebrate the political and class power of unions and think of the relationships, skills, confidence and experience they nurture only as a nice bonus. In truth, they are integral. In a world where capitalism thrives on our atomisation, competition and self-doubt, forming caring and supportive friendships is defiance, and believing in ourselves is radical and powerful. Collectivism builds our power within the workplace and society, but it also builds something inside us. As Dawn Butler, Labour MP and formerly a full-time union officer, tells me: 'The trade union ethos . . . is a big part of why I'm now an MP.' She highlights the pride she still feels, decades later, in a successful campaign to secure a wage increase and adequate equipment for cleaners. 'I learned from that work and I use it in my campaigning to fight for the rights of all in society, including my constituents.'

The time spent in a union is formative, and its effects lifelong. If it awakens a political consciousness, if it broadens a worker's horizons, if it nurtures human connections and all the potential they bring, then it has done its job. Every time a new trade unionist is formed, the working class grows just a little bit stronger.

Resources

When deciding which union to join, your first port of call should be to find out whether your workplace already recognises one and/or whether your coworkers are already members of one. It is always best to join the union already represented in your workplace. But if that does not apply to you, I hope the following list might help.

Below is a list of unions, organised roughly by job type. This list is not exhaustive and its categorisations are not definitive: many will overlap with each other and there are many more (particularly for those in very small sectors or specialist roles) than I am able to list here. But I hope it is a useful starting point from which to do your own research about which union is best for you.

For any worker regardless of role
Community
GMB
Industrial Workers of the World (IWW)
Unite

For gig economy, insecure, charity or self-employed workers
The Independent Workers of Great Britain (IWGB)
United Voices of the World (UVW)

RESOURCES

For the arts and culture
Artists' Union England
Equity
Musicians' Union
National Union of Journalists (NUJ)

For transport workers
Associated Society of Locomotive Engineers and Firemen
(ASLEF)
National Union of Rail, Maritime and Transport Workers
(RMT)

For hospitality workers
Bakers, Food and Allied Workers' Union (BFAWU)
Unite Hospitality

For medical workers
British Medical Association (BMA)
Royal College of Midwives
Royal College of Nursing

For communications, telecoms and postal workers
Communication Workers Union (CWU)

For education workers
Educational Institute of Scotland (EIS)
National Education Union (NEU)
University and College Union (UCU)

For emergency services workers
Fire Brigades Union (FBU)

For public services workers
Public and Commercial Services Union (PCS)
UNISON

For retail and distribution workers
Union of Shop Distributive and Allied Workers (USDAW)

For civil servants, managerial roles, engineers, finance and others
Prospect
Financial Services Union

For the unemployed
Unite Community

Thanks to our Patreon Subscribers:

Lia Lilith de Oliveira
Andrew Perry

Who have shown generosity and comradeship in support of our publishing.

Check out the other perks you get by subscribing to our Patreon – visit patreon.com/plutopress.

Subscriptions start from £3 a month.

The Pluto Press Newsletter

Hello friend of Pluto!

Want to stay on top of the best radical books we publish?

Then sign up to be the first to hear about our new books, as well as special events, podcasts and videos.

You'll also get 50% off your first order with us when you sign up.

Come and join us!

Go to bit.ly/PlutoNewsletter